OPPOSING VIEWPOINTS® SERIES

The Politics of
Water Scarcity

Other Books of Related Interest

Opposing Viewpoints Series
Dictatorships
Global Resources
Global Sustainability
Human Rights
The United Nations
Water

At Issue Series
Adaptation and Climate Change
Can Glacier and Ice Melt Be Reversed?
Food Insecurity
Should There Be an International Climate Treaty?
Will the World Run Out of Fresh Water?
World Hunger

Current Controversies Series
Aid to Africa
Conserving the Environment
Developing Nations
Food
Global Warming
The Global Food Crisis

> "Congress shall make no law … abridging the freedom of speech, or of the press."

First Amendment to the US Constitution

The basic foundation of our democracy is the First Amendment guarantee of freedom of expression. The Opposing Viewpoints series is dedicated to the concept of this basic freedom and the idea that it is more important to practice it than to enshrine it.

OPPOSING
VIEWPOINTS®
SERIES

The Politics of Water Scarcity

Susan Nichols, Book Editor

GREENHAVEN
PUBLISHING

Published in 2018 by Greenhaven Publishing, LLC
353 3rd Avenue, Suite 255, New York, NY 10010

Library of Congress Cataloging-in-Publication Data

Names: Nichols, Susan, editor.
Title: The politics of water scarcity / edited by Susan Nichols.
Description: New York : Greenhaven Publishing, 2018. | Series: Opposing viewpoints
| Includes bibliographical references and index. | Audience: Grades 9-12.
Identifiers: LCCN ISBN 9781534500549 (library bound) | ISBN 9781534500525 (pbk.)
Subjects: LCSH: Water-supply--Juvenile literature. | Water consumption-
-Juvenile literature. | Water conservation--Juvenile literature.
Classification: LCC TD348.P655 2018 | DDC 333.91'16--dc23

Manufactured in the United States of America

Website: http://greenhavenpublishing.com

Contents

The Importance of Opposing Viewpoints   **11**

Introduction   **14**

Chapter 1: Do We Take Clean Water for Granted?

Chapter Preface   **17**

1. We Can No Longer Take Water for Granted   **19**
   Paul Alois

2. Our Drinking Water Is Safe   **27**
   Daniel Moss

3. Water Is Not a Human Right   **34**
   Louie Glinzak

4. Water Accessibility Affects All Parts of Society   **39**
   Moses Mozart Dzawu

5. We Must Work Together to Solve Drought Problems   **43**
   Daniel Polk

Periodical and Internet Sources Bibliography   **53**

Chapter 2: What Is Causing Water Scarcity?

Chapter Preface   **55**

1. Fracking Contributes to Water Scarcity   **57**
   Joshua Pringle

2. To Solve Water Scarcity, Slow the Human Population Growth   **63**
   Robert Engelman

3. Water Scarcity Is Caused by Excessive Extraction of Groundwater   **70**
   Feng Hao

4. Groundwater Overdrafting Must be Regulated   **76**
   Tara Moran, Janny Choy and Carolina Sanchez

5. Water Scarcity is the Result of Mismanagement   **85**
   Prasenjit Chowdhury

6. A Combination of Solutions Must Be Used to Solve   **89**
the Problem of Water Scarcity
Nadia Halim

Periodical and Internet Sources Bibliography   **95**

Chapter 3: How Is Water Used as a Political Tool?

Chapter Preface   **97**

1. Global Water Shortages Pose Threat of Terror and War   **99**
Suzanne Goldenberg

2. Water Scarcity Leads to Internal Strife for Nations   **105**
Pallava Bagla

3. Water Scarcity in Central Asia May Lead to Conflict   **111**
Emily Singer Hurvitz

4. Water Can Be a Source of Disagreement Among   **115**
Neighboring Nations
The Third Pole

5. Water Scarcity Is a Product of Flawed International   **121**
Agreements
Cyril Ferrand

6. Water Access Contributes to a Region's Stability   **125**
Christopher Tatlock

Periodical and Internet Sources Bibliography   **133**

Chapter 4: What Is the Solution for Reducing Water Scarcity?

Chapter Preface   **135**

1. Stop Population Growth to End Water Scarcity   **137**
Laurie Mazur

2. Learn Nature's Lessons for Water Conservation   **143**
Stephanie Vierra

3. We Should Learn to Replicate Natural Desalination   **147**
Aditya Sood

4. Technology and Engineering Can Fix Water   **152**
   Scarcity in China
   Yu Yang, Lei Yin, and Qingzong Zhang

5. It's Time to Declare War on Water Scarcity   **166**
   Gabriel Wong

6. Save Water Through Irrigation Innovation   **176**
   Mary Kay Magistad

Periodical and Internet Sources Bibliography   **181**

For Further Discussion   **182**

Organizations to Contact   **184**

Bibliography of Books   **187**

Index   **189**

The Importance of Opposing Viewpoints

Perhaps every generation experiences a period in time in which the populace seems especially polarized, starkly divided on the important issues of the day and gravitating toward the far ends of the political spectrum and away from a consensus-facilitating middle ground. The world that today's students are growing up in and that they will soon enter into as active and engaged citizens is deeply fragmented in just this way. Issues relating to terrorism, immigration, women's rights, minority rights, race relations, health care, taxation, wealth and poverty, the environment, policing, military intervention, the proper role of government—in some ways, perennial issues that are freshly and uniquely urgent and vital with each new generation—are currently roiling the world.

If we are to foster a knowledgeable, responsible, active, and engaged citizenry among today's youth, we must provide them with the intellectual, interpretive, and critical-thinking tools and experience necessary to make sense of the world around them and of the all-important debates and arguments that inform it. After all, the outcome of these debates will in large measure determine the future course, prospects, and outcomes of the world and its peoples, particularly its youth. If they are to become successful members of society and productive and informed citizens, students need to learn how to evaluate the strengths and weaknesses of someone else's arguments, how to sift fact from opinion and fallacy, and how to test the relative merits and validity of their own opinions against the known facts and the best possible available information. The landmark series Opposing Viewpoints has been providing students with just such critical-thinking skills and exposure to the debates surrounding society's most urgent contemporary issues for many years, and it continues to serve this essential role with undiminished commitment, care, and rigor.

The key to the series's success in achieving its goal of sharpening students' critical-thinking and analytic skills resides in its title—

Opposing Viewpoints. In every intriguing, compelling, and engaging volume of this series, readers are presented with the widest possible spectrum of distinct viewpoints, expert opinions, and informed argumentation and commentary, supplied by some of today's leading academics, thinkers, analysts, politicians, policy makers, economists, activists, change agents, and advocates. Every opinion and argument anthologized here is presented objectively and accorded respect. There is no editorializing in any introductory text or in the arrangement and order of the pieces. No piece is included as a "straw man," an easy ideological target for cheap point-scoring. As wide and inclusive a range of viewpoints as possible is offered, with no privileging of one particular political ideology or cultural perspective over another. It is left to each individual reader to evaluate the relative merits of each argument—as he or she sees it, and with the use of ever-growing critical-thinking skills—and grapple with his or her own assumptions, beliefs, and perspectives to determine how convincing or successful any given argument is and how the reader's own stance on the issue may be modified or altered in response to it.

This process is facilitated and supported by volume, chapter, and selection introductions that provide readers with the essential context they need to begin engaging with the spotlighted issues, with the debates surrounding them, and with their own perhaps shifting or nascent opinions on them. In addition, guided reading and discussion questions encourage readers to determine the authors' point of view and purpose, interrogate and analyze the various arguments and their rhetoric and structure, evaluate the arguments' strengths and weaknesses, test their claims against available facts and evidence, judge the validity of the reasoning, and bring into clearer, sharper focus the reader's own beliefs and conclusions and how they may differ from or align with those in the collection or those of their classmates.

Research has shown that reading comprehension skills improve dramatically when students are provided with compelling, intriguing, and relevant "discussable" texts. The subject matter of these collections could not be more compelling, intriguing, or urgently relevant to today's students and the world they are poised to inherit. The anthologized articles and the reading and discussion questions that are included with them also provide the basis for stimulating, lively, and passionate classroom debates. Students who are compelled to anticipate objections to their own argument and identify the flaws in those of an opponent read more carefully, think more critically, and steep themselves in relevant context, facts, and information more thoroughly. In short, using discussable text of the kind provided by every single volume in the Opposing Viewpoints series encourages close reading, facilitates reading comprehension, fosters research, strengthens critical thinking, and greatly enlivens and energizes classroom discussion and participation. The entire learning process is deepened, extended, and strengthened.

For all of these reasons, Opposing Viewpoints continues to be exactly the right resource at exactly the right time—when we most need to provide readers with the critical-thinking tools and skills that will not only serve them well in school but also in their careers and their daily lives as decision-making family members, community members, and citizens. This series encourages respectful engagement with and analysis of opposing viewpoints and fosters a resulting increase in the strength and rigor of one's own opinions and stances. As such, it helps make readers "future ready," and that readiness will pay rich dividends for the readers themselves, for the citizenry, for our society, and for the world at large.

Introduction

By 2030, the world is projected to
face a 40% global water deficit."—
The United Nations World Water
Development Report 2015, "Water
for a Sustainable World."

Water has always been recognized as an essential element necessary for human survival. Most ancient and classical civilizations paid homage to water gods and deities, such as Poseidon in Greek mythology and Belisama and Lir, deities of water bodies in Celtic mythology. Schoolchildren learn such astounding facts as that the human body is composed mostly of water, and that human life is not sustainable without water.

They also learn the fact that water makes up 70% of the earth's surface. In fact, from space, the Earth looks like a blue marble because of the oceans and lakes that cover its surface.

However, the United Nations has projected that if drastic changes are not made, then by 2030 humans will only have 60% of the water that they need. But when there is so much water on Earth, how can there suddenly not be enough to sustain human life?

The danger of a global water shortage is already being felt in many parts of the world. Many communities struggle to find fresh, drinkable water. The world population is currently at 7.4 billion people, but more than one billion of them do not have access to safe water. This leads to malnutrition, illness, disease, and a whole host of other problems. Without water, communities cannot produce items needed for their own survival, such as food and clothing. What is causing this to happen?

This resource offers viewpoints that explain some of the factors causing water scarcity. Some experts believe it is climate change, while others believe it is overconsumption and human waste. Some people think this is an issue that third-world and underdeveloped countries must cope with; however, the problem is closer to home than some may realize.

For example, the state of California has been experiencing a significant drought, which has caused the price of water to increase. Businesses and farms are going out of business, and trees are dying. The state has determined that it can do much to reduce human consumption of water.

In April 2015, Governor Jerry Brown issued a mandate that restricted statewide water use, in an attempt to reduce water usage in urban areas by 25 percent. The mandate was the first time in the history of California that such restrictions had to be issued. Some of the restrictions include stopping cities from watering median strips on highways, as well as removing large, grassy areas throughout the state and replacing them with drought-resistant landscaping. Individuals were also called upon to stop using appliances that waste water and replace them with high-efficiency substitutes.

Whether the restrictions will work has yet to be determined. However, California's success is crucial, as it is the state from which most other states in the nation import their produce. If California fails, then this will have a negative impact on all Americans. Many Californians thought that the restrictions were unfair, but as Governor Brown said plainly, "It's a different world. We have to act differently."

Opposing Viewpoints: The Politics of Water Scarcity explores just how different the world is now in relation to the water crisis, in chapters with titles such as "Do We Take Clean Water for Granted?", "What Is Causing Water Scarcity?", "How Is Water Used as a Political Tool?", and "What Is the Solution for Reducing Water Scarcity?" It's a different world, but in order to understand the solution, we must first examine the problem from different angles.

OPPOSING
VIEWPOINTS®
SERIES

CHAPTER 1

Do We Take Clean Water for Granted?

Chapter Preface

In most parts of North America, people understand water in a simple way: they know that when they open their sink faucets, water will pour out—and that water will be safe to drink and use. The fact that this is not the case in many other parts of the Western hemisphere, and in many parts of the globe, is not well understood.

We have become used to having safe water, and the long history of the civil engineering, filtration technology, and public health work that made it a reality is unknown to us. In fact, some would argue that it is a privilege to have easy and affordable access to clean water.

In the United States, an uproar was triggered by the case of Flint, Michigan, in 2015. In an effort to save the city from its severe financial problems, the government had approved a plan to temporarily provide water to Flint from an alternative source. Its original source had been Lake Huron; he alternative source was the Flint River. The water from the Flint River was so corrosive that it had to be treated before it could be piped to the city. The Detroit Water and Sewage Department warned that this was not a safe plan, but the city proceeded anyway.

The city of Flint began using Flint River water in 2014. Residents soon complained about the quality of the water: it tasted bad, it caused people to break out in rashes, and it contained bacteria. Two advisories were issued in August and September of 2014 for people to boil water before using it because e-coli and coliform bacteria were detected in the water. Cases of legionnaire's disease began to rise, and residents complained to government officials that their water was discolored and even brown.

In September 2015, a Flint-based pediatrician, Dr. Mona Hanna-Attisha, provided startling numbers: she reported a severe rise in lead levels in the blood of children she tested. Lead poisoning causes a whole host of developmental and life-threatening problems, and Hanna-Attisha aggressively demanded that this be investigated. One month later, a public health emergency was declared, and the nation was horrified at what was happening in a typical American city: that people were being poisoned and made sick by their drinking water.

The residents of Flint, Michigan, have been receiving bottled water, but the emergency has taken its toll on the city. The issue is still not resolved and it may be years before the full extent of the damage is understood.

Public health and engineering developments of the last century have perhaps made us feel comfortable about the water that comes out of our faucets. But do we take it for granted that our drinking water is safe? And do we assume that we will always have plenty of it? The viewpoints in this chapter tackle these questions.

| "*Population growth and groundwater depletion present the two most significant dangers to global water stability.*"

We Can No Longer Take Water for Granted

Paul Alois

In the following viewpoint, Paul Alois explains the many ways in which water is becoming more scarce around the world. The numbers he provides to substantiate his observations are startling, such as the sharp increase in the global population—which in turn, puts more stress and demand on the water supply. Most helpfully, Alois points out the different consequences of a reduced water supply, such as its impact on food sources and its potential to cause political and military conflicts. Alois is a Ph.D candidate in international affairs at the City University of New York. He has previously worked as a researcher and writer for the World Bank and the Arlington Institute, a nonprofit think tank that examines national security in light of various forces of global change.

"Global Water Crisis Overview," by Paul Alois, The Arlington Institute, April, 2007. Reprinted by permission.

As you read, consider the following questions:

1. What are some of the major factors that have contributed to water scarcity?
2. What are some of the most significant consequences of a decreased water supply?
3. How have manufacturing and industry, rather than agriculture, contributed to water scarcity?

Water, simply put, makes the existence of the human race on this planet possible. With few exceptions, water has always been a natural resource that people take for granted. Today, the situation has changed.

The World Bank reports that 80 countries now have water shortages and 2 billion people lack access to clean water. More disturbingly, the World Health Organization has reported that 1 billion people lack enough water to simply meet their basic needs.

Population growth and groundwater depletion present the two most significant dangers to global water stability. In the last century, the human population has increased from 1.7 billion people to 6.6 billion people, while the total amount of potable water has slightly decreased. Much of the population growth and economic development experienced in the last fifty years has been supported by subterranean water reserves called groundwater. These nonrenewable reserves, an absolutely essential aspect of the modern world, are being consumed at an unsustainable rate.

The Present Supply and Usage of Water

Humanity has approximately 11 trillion cubic meters of freshwater at its disposal. Groundwater aquifers contain over 95% of this water, while rain, rivers, and lakes make up the remaining 5%. Approximately 1,700 m³ of water exists for every person on the planet, an alarming low number. According to the Water Stress Index, a region with less than 1,700 m³ per capita is considered "water stressed".

The global supply is not distributed evenly around the planet, nor is water equally available at all times throughout the year. Many areas of the world have seriously inadequate access to water, and many places with high annual averages experience alternating seasons of drought and monsoons.

Water usage differs highly between developing countries and developed ones. Developing countries use 90% of their water for agriculture, 5% for industry, and 5% for urban areas. Developed countries use 45% of their water for agriculture, 45% for industry, and 10% for urban areas.

In the last century water usage per person doubled, even as the total population tripled, creating a situation today where many areas of the world are consuming water at an unsustainable rate.

Increasing Demand

The agricultural sector, by far the largest consumer of freshwater resources, accounts for 70% global consumption. Irrigation consumes most of the water in the agricultural sector, and has become an integral part of modern civilization because of access to groundwater aquifers. Once farmers were freed from relying on rain to water their crops, highly efficient commercial farming became increasingly common. This innovation also underpinned the Green Revolution, which dramatically increased crop production throughout the third world in the 1960s. Unfortunately, water is being drawn from many of these aquifers faster than it is being replaced.

The industrial sector accounts for 22% of global water consumption; this number will grow in the coming decades as the developing world industrializes. The needs of industry tend to take precedence over agriculture for simple economic reasons. 1,000 tons of water will produce 1 ton of wheat, which is worth $200. 1,000 tons of water in the industrial sector, however, will generate $14,000 worth of goods. On a per ton basis, industry creates 70 times more wealth. Despite its economic benefits, intense water use by industry has led to serious pollution that is beginning to create problems worldwide.

The residential sector uses the remaining 8% of the total water supply. Although this sector only accounts for a small percentage of overall use, it always takes precedence over industry and agriculture. In the last fifty years the world's urban population has exploded, and by 2010 50% of the people on the planet will live in cities. In addition to the simple increase in population, per person consumption of water has risen. As more people begin utilizing modern luxuries like flush toilets, showers, and washing machines, the demand created by the residential sector will increase dramatically.

Water Pollution

The companion of modernization has always been pollution. In developing countries that are just entering the industrial age, water pollution presents a serious problem. According to United Nations Environmental Program (UNEP), "in developing countries, rivers downstream from major cities are little cleaner than open sewers". The UNEP also reports that 1.2 billion people are being affected by polluted water, and that dirty water contributes to 15 million child deaths every year. In recent years, scientists have become aware of the problems involved with the contamination of groundwater. Aquifers move very slowly, so once they are polluted it takes decades or centuries for them to cleanse themselves.

Food production contributes significantly to water contamination. When nitrogen fertilizer is applied to a field, the water runoff will contain excess amounts of nitrates. Nitrates have been shown to have a very harmful effect on plant and animal life, can cause miscarriages, and can harm infant development. The industrial livestock business also presents a serious danger to water systems. The disposal of vast amounts of animal feces destroys nearby ecosystems and is very hazardous to humans.

Water pollution is reaching epic proportions. In the U.S. 40% of rivers and lakes are considered too polluted to support normal activities. In China 80% of the rivers are so polluted that fish cannot survive in them. In Japan 30% of groundwater has been contaminated by industrial pollution. The Ganges River, which supports around 500 million people, is considered one of the most polluted rivers in the world. And the list goes on…

Food Scarcity

According to the International Food Policy Research Institute (IFPRI), if current water consumption trends continue, by 2025 the agricultural sector will experience serious water shortages. The IFPRI estimates that crop losses due to water scarcity could be as high as 350 million metric tons per year, slightly more than the entire crop yield of the U.S. This massive water crisis will be caused by water contamination, diverting water for industrial purposes, and the depletion of aquifers. Climate change may also play a part. The Himalayan glaciers, which feed the rivers that support billions of people, are shrinking in size every year. Their disappearance would cause a major humanitarian disaster.

The greatest danger to global food security comes from aquifer depletion. Aquifers are an essential source of water for food production, and they are being overdrawn in the western U.S., northern Iran, north-central China, India, Mexico, Australia, and numerous other locations. Additionally, many aquifers are contaminated each year by pollution and seawater intrusion.

Despite their importance, data on underground water reservoirs remains imprecise. There is little evidence regarding how many aquifers actually exist, and the depth of known aquifers is often a mystery. However, it is clear that water from these sources takes centuries to replenish, and that they are being consumed at a highly unsustainable rate.

International Conflict

According to the UNEP, there are 263 rivers in the world that either cross or mark international boundaries. The basins fed by these rivers account for 60% of the world's above ground freshwater. Of these 263 rivers, 158 have no international legislation, and many are the source of conflict.

Water has always been a central issue in Arab-Israeli situation. Ariel Sharon once said the Six Days War actually began the day that Israel stopped Syria from diverting the Jordan River in 1964. Decades later, the Egyptian military came close to staging a coup against Egyptian president Anwar Sadat, who had proposed diverting some of the Nile's water to Israel as part of a peace plan.

The Nile River, which runs through Ethiopia, Sudan, and Egypt, exemplifies the potential for future water conflicts. The banks of the Nile River support one of most densely populated areas on the planet. In the next fifty years the number of people dependent on the Nile could double, creating a serious water crisis in the region. The Nile is not governed by any multilateral treaties, and Egypt would not shrink from using military strength to guarantee its future access to water.

The potential for water conflicts are less likely outside the Middle East, but never the less there are many problematic areas. The Mekong River is the lifeblood of South East Asia, but it begins in one of the most water poor countries on Earth: China. The Indus River separates Pakistan and India, and aquifer depletion by Indian farmers has one of the highest rates in the world. U.S.-Mexican relations are already strained over water use on their mutual border. The Niger River basin in West-Central Africa runs through five countries. Surging populations coupled with decreasing rainfall in the region seriously threaten water security for millions of people.

Although the specter of international water wars can seem very real, in the last 50 years there have only been 7 conflicts over water outside the Middle East. While a global water crisis has the potential to tear international relations at the seams, it also has the potential to force the global community into a new spirit of cooperation.

Solutions

The oceans contain 97% of the world's water. Desalination technology transforms the vast amount of salt water in the Earth's oceans into freshwater fit for human consumption. There are approximately 7,500 desalination plants in the world, 60% of which are in the Middle East. The global desalination industry has a capacity of approximately 28 million m3, less than 1% of global demand. Desalination is an expensive and energy intensive technology, and currently only wealthy countries with serious water shortages consider it a viable option. However, a recent innovation using nanotechnology has the potential to decrease the cost of desalination by 75%, making it a more viable option.

While irrigation accounts for approximately one third of all global water consumption, numerous studies have shown that approximately half of the water used in irrigation is lost through evaporation or seepage. Drip irrigation technology offers a far more water-efficient way of farming. Drip irrigation techniques involve using a series of pipes to distribute water in a very controlled manner. By using this method farmers have the ability to give their crops the exact amount of water needed. Despite its many benefits, drip irrigation is not being widely implemented. While the technology is not sophisticated or expensive, it is beyond the means of the poorest farmers who need it most. It is also not being used by many farmers in water-rich countries because the potential savings are less than the cost of implementing the technology.

In many countries water shortages are exacerbated or even caused by governmental mismanagement, political infighting, and outright corruption. International organizations like the World Trade Organization (WTO) often suggest that privatization of water management services would alleviate many of these problems. It has been shown that privatizing utilities frequently increases efficiency, innovation, and maintenance. However, privatization rarely has an effect on corruption, and often disadvantages the poor.

Other technical solutions like rainwater capture, water-free toilets, and water reclamation offer people the possibility of effective conservation. Market-oriented solutions such as water tariffs, pricing groundwater, and increasing fines against industries that pollute could be adopted. There are also a number of viable trade solutions. Freshwater could be traded internationally by using pipelines and enormous plastic bags. Despite this plethora of potential solutions, there is no substitute for simply consuming less.

Conclusion

In the coming decades, water crises will likely become increasingly common. If the population continues to grow at a rate of 1 billion people every 15 years, the Earth's capacity to support human life will be severely strained. Population growth notwithstanding, the current supply of water is being degraded by pollution, overdrawing, and climate change. It is not too late to guarantee a safe supply of water for everyone alive today and for all future generations; although to do so would require an unprecedented level of international cooperation, trust, and compassion.

> *"Water consumers want results—clean water gushing from their faucet. They wonder: Is my city a leader or a hazard to my health?"*

Our Drinking Water Is Safe

Daniel Moss

In the following viewpoint, Daniel Moss addresses the concern that many Americans have about the safety of their drinking water. However, he advises readers that it is possible for municipal systems to provide safe drinking water. While the situation in Flint, Michigan, is a tragedy, it is mostly a result of poor management decisions. In contrast, there are many more examples of urban areas, such as New York City, that have capably and ably provided water that is not only safe to drink but that even tastes good to the city's millions of residents. Moss works with Latin American and Caribbean water utilities to protect their water sources and strengthen resiliency in the face of climate change.

"Can We Trust Our Drinking Water?" by Daniel Moss, On the Commons, February 17, 2016. http://www.onthecommons.org/magazine/can-we-trust-our-drinking-water. Licensed under CC BY SA 3.0.

As you read, consider the following questions:

1. How was the crisis in Flint, Michigan, mostly a result of bad management?
2. How have major cities like New York been able to provide safe drinking water?
3. How common is it for disease and illness to spread through the public water system?

With the unfolding horror of Flint's water crisis, filling a glass of tap water suddenly feels risky.

Throughout history, water quality has been a challenge—cholera, dysentery, and other diseases have felled great cities. Today, more than a billion people remain without safe water access around the world.

And yet, internationally, water is now recognized as a human right, and how to manage it equitably and sustainably is highlighted in climate change agreements as well as the United Nations Sustainable Development Goals. Climate change and energy conservation imperatives are driving changes. As cities learn to protect source water, capture rainwater, recycle grey water, involve the public and establish watershed committees, creativity in urban water management is taking off.

In the end, though, water consumers want results—clean water gushing from their faucet. They wonder: Is my city a leader or a hazard to my health?

Flint can be looked at two ways. It may be an exception, a story of a callous governor making cost-saving decisions at the expense of Flint's mostly black and brown children. Or it could signal the beginning of a systemic breakdown within the more than 50,000 water utilities in the United States.

So far, despite decaying infrastructure and budget pressures, water utilities have delivered on their promise of healthy water. Many cities have taken positive steps to avoid what has happened in Flint.

Flint is preceded by plenty of disasters, most the result of bad management decisions, that have eroded public confidence and prompted action. In 2014, algae blooms, fed by heavy nitrate use, ruined the water supply in Toledo, Ohio. A dramatic chemical spill in Charleston, West Virginia, left that city's water undrinkable. These calamities are free advertising for the United States' $13 billion bottled water market.

But before giving up on public water, there's evidence to consider. As tragic as the news is out of Flint, said American Water Works Association Communications Director Greg Kail, almost all of the nation's water utilities are in compliance with the Safe Water Drinking Act's Lead and Copper Rule. The utilities would have to acknowledge any violations in annual Consumer Confidence Reports. "In the vast majority of cases," said Kail, "water professionals discharge their duties with seriousness and protect public health. When something like Flint occurs, it strengthens their commitment."

On the heels of Flint, the Massachusetts Water Resources Authority (MWRA) and New York City's Department of Environmental Protection (DEP) circulated reassuring letters to legislators and customers describing their water quality measures. The DEP proactively distributes 1,000 test kits per year to customers to collect household-level data on lead and other contaminants. The MWRA and DEP both rely on feedback from customers, what Stephen Estes-Smargiassi, the MWRA's director of Planning and Sustainability, described as "building confidence at the retail level. We want customers to have a good feeling about their water after they interact with us." The MWRA, like many water utilities, tracks and publishes water quality data on its website, and has a water quality hot-line with a public health professional to respond to inquiries. In Flint, the switch to a new water source was not disclosed, and customer complaints were routinely ignored.

In-house and regulatory safeguards shouldn't stop alert citizens from making their concerns known at City Hall, but in the vast majority of cases, public urban water meets EPA standards. While the American Society of Civil Engineers' Report Card for America's Infrastructure gives the nation's drinking-water infrastructure a "D" grade—raising red flags about the $3.2 trillion the United States needs by 2020 to upgrade water infrastructure nationwide—the report also says that "outbreaks of disease attributable to drinking water are rare." While that is not a ringing endorsement, healthy water advocates can point their public officials to smart cities that manage their water well, investing in transparent governance, "grey infrastructure"—piping and treatment—and "green infrastructure"—rehabilitating ecosystems to ensure water quality and quantity.

New York City's water system is emblematic of this trend, frequently featured at water-management conferences around the world. Its innovative planning began in the 1800s with gravity-fed pipes carrying pristine water to the city from the Catskill and Delaware watersheds. In the 1980s, facing contamination from industrial agriculture and encroaching suburbanization, rather than build a $6 billion treatment plant, the water utility pioneered urban-rural collaboration in what came to be known as "payments for environmental services." In return for healthy drinking water, the city transferred cash to rural areas to improve animal-waste management on farms and sanitation in towns.

Although New York City likes to claim title to the "champagne" of drinking water, in 2014 it was edged out by Boston in the American Water Works Annual Tap Water Taste Test. Similar to New York City, Boston keeps water clean at its source. Whereas New York primarily forges land-use agreements with private landowners, Boston concentrates on protecting public lands in collaboration with state agencies. Conserving the forest around the Quabbin and Wachusetts reservoirs means that, to achieve Environmental Protection Agency (EPA) standards, Boston water requires only minimal treatment.

The city's good tasting water isn't just an aesthetic bonus: It means that when water smells bad or is discolored, customers call the utility to complain.

Economic Commodity or Human Right?

Consider water: Should it be understood primarily as an economic commodity or as a fundamental human right? Fresh water is not like most other environmental goods or services. It is *sine qua non* (fundamental to ecosystemic and human existence) and *sui generis* (there is no substitute).

These features are universal but are not uniform. Yet for a range of reasons it took the United Nations General Assembly until 2010 to affirm a fundamental human right to water.

Given the U.N.'s rather recent endorsement, it surprises many observers that the Catholic Church has taken a moral position on this issue since at least 2003—insisting, in no uncertain terms, that fresh water is a unique and essential substance for human life; that it is a gift from God; and that therefore access to fresh water should be considered a fundamental human right.

[...]

The Catholic Church's global, public endorsement of the right to water is but one example. There are many others.

In Detroit, where questions of water and justice remain visible and vexed, support for disenfranchised people can—and should—take practical, embodied forms.

One compelling and recent example comes from Islamic Relief U.S.A., which along with the Michigan Muslim Community Council donated $100,000 to defray water bill payments for impoverished Detroit residents. "It is important to us in our faith to help our neighbors," said the CEO of Islamic Relief USA in January 2015.

To be sure, religious cosmologies or moral principles will not save the planet on their own. But they are crucial, often vibrant repositories of values and practices that might just help to make the world a more just, sustainable place—one municipality or human right at a time.

"Water: Economic Commodity or Human Right?" by Christiana Z. Peppard, The University of Chicago, April 2, 2015.

Upstream and downstream, watersheds are home to competing economic interests, many of which can compromise water quality. Governments have used both carrots and sticks to ensure responsible water and land use that yield clean water. After stirring a hornet's nest of angry farmers with strict regulation enforcement, New York's water utility switched tactics and offered direct aid to farmers who voluntarily engaged in watershed-friendly farming.

A similar challenge emerged in the Midwest. Iowa's $30 billion grain trade is fattened by a multimillion-dollar infusion of chemical fertilizers, only a portion of which actually ends up fertilizing corn and soy plants. Much of the rest of it is washed into waterways like the Raccoon River, a principal Des Moines water source. Bill Stowe, the chief executive of Des Moines Water Works, said that the state failed in its efforts to get farmers to willingly reduce nitrate runoff.

"It's very clear to me," Stowe said in a New York Times article, "that traditional, industrial agriculture has no real interest in taking the steps that are necessary to radically change their operations in a way that will protect our drinking water." Treating the nitrate-filled water to potable water standards isn't cheap, so in 2015, the water utility served farmers the bill via a lawsuit against two upstream counties. While this may sound like the makings of an urban-rural civil war, the lawsuit has set in motion an important public debate in Iowa about who ought to pay for clean water.

Self-taxing may seem unlikely today in many communities today, but California voters in 2014 approved a $7.5 billion bond to repair and replace aging and vulnerable water infrastructure. Parched lawns, made more visible by Governor Jerry Brown's vocal leadership on water conservation and climate change, shook voters from complacency; water can't be taken for granted. The bond meant that water bills will likely spike, but voters put thirst before wallets.

Funds will be used to, among other things, shore up water reliability, meet safe drinking-water standards, and clean up groundwater. Some $260 million will go to the State Water Pollution Control Revolving Fund's Small Community Grant Fund, run by the State Water Resources Control Board. In the Bay Area, a 2002 voter-approved bond has helped the San Francisco Public Utility Commission blend groundwater with Sierra Nevada snow melt and incentivize San Francisco builders to collect and treat water onsite, part of what Paula Kehoe, director of Water Resources at the San Francisco Public Utilities Commission, describes as "a new water paradigm."

Such a paradigm may not come without a struggle. When United Water won the contract to manage Atlanta's water system in 1999, they halved the workforce and increased rates. Brown and orange water dripping from city faucets led to boil-only alerts. Then Mayor Shirley Franklin canceled the contract in 2003 and restored municipal management of the water system. Around the world, citizens are forcing re-examination of private contracts and pressuring city governments to take back control of water services. Faced with rate hikes without service improvements, communities question how returning profits to private shareholders squares with managing water for the public good. The Transnational Institute's remunicipalization tracker reports that in the past 15 years, 235 cities in 37 countries have brought water systems under public control.

Flint's tragedy has moved the country like no other water crisis. When one water utility betrays the public trust, Estes-Smargiassi said, "it damages confidence everywhere." The injuries in Flint will persist well beyond its scarred children. It may be some time before families feel reassured enough to drink from their tap. And yet every day and everywhere, there are examples of committed water workers and forward-thinking city officials demonstrating that, with enough investment and public oversight, water can be managed for the public good.

> "*As water is becoming scarcer we will need to reevaluate how we use and treat this precious resource.*"

Water Is Not a Human Right

Louie Glinzak

In the following viewpoint, Louie Glinzak takes an interesting and controversial stance. He argues that one should not view safe drinking water as a human right, but rather as a commodity like anything else. In other words, water is something that people should pay for, rather than something that they are owed by their governments. Glinzak explains that water has historically been provided by rulers and governments throughout history, but in our modern era, the private sector—that is, business and industry—could have an important role to play. Glinzak's opinions are informed by a number of influences, including the stance of the Catholic Church, modern theorists, and his own historical readings. Glinzak is an attorney and a judge advocate in the United States Marine Corps.

"Water: A Right or a Commodity?" by Louie Glinzak, Acton Institute, July 12, 2011. Reprinted by permission.

As you read, consider the following questions:

1. Why should water not be considered a basic human right?
2. What is Glinak's intent in sharing the example of ancient Roman water policies?
3. What is the role of the private sector and business in providing drinking water to the public?

W ater is becoming scarcer and even more of a necessity than it was before. And while stories of water scarcity typically occur in underdeveloped, arid countries, the United States and other developed countries must realize they are no longer exceptions and must take into consideration the importance of water and the allocation of its use.

A recent article in the *Wall Street Journal* explores the severe lack of water in Palm Beach, Florida. Residents are restricted to once-a-week watering schedules for lawns and plants, however, not all residents are abiding by restrictions whereas many owners of large estates are continuing an excessive use of water. The disparity in water usage has created a disgruntled community in West Palm Beach.

While residents in the U.S. are disagreeing over water usage for landscape purposes, many throughout the world are dying of thirst, thus, putting forth the question, do communities need to reevaluate their water use? Grass, and green luscious landscapes that are found in more moderate climates are not natural to southern Florida, so is it moral for residents to obtain a landscape, requiring a large use of water, that isn't even native to an area?

Water scarcity has become a cause for concern in the United Kingdom, and Egypt and Ethiopia have been battling over the share of the Nile's water reserves. Many countries and local communities are now forced to take into consideration their long term use of water.

In past blog posts I've taken a look at the water crisis and with Italians recently deciding to repeal a law that required water to be treated as a commodity, an explanation of my previous argument in support for treating water as a commodity is needed. My last post was missing an important moral case for the privatization of water that needs to be addressed.

In his essay, "Thirst: A Short History of Drinking Water" James Salzman analyzes how different civilizations throughout history provided drinking water. Jewish law, according to Salzman, treated water as a common property resource, not an open access resource. Priority was given according to use, giving drinking water the highest priority. While water, which came from a well made possible by human labor, was for community use only, nobody was turned away who was in need of drinking water.

Rome is a great example of how water resources were allocated when a water supply and sanitation system existed. There was a public water source, known as the lacus, where Romans could collect water for free. When using the lacus, Romans had to use their own manual labor to transport the water from the lacus to their homes. However, there was also a private water supply where Romans could pay to have water brought into their homes through a pipe system.

The "right to thirst," as explained by Salzman, is recognized by both the Romans and the Jewish law. Salzman explains every human has a right to water, and both civilizations understand that right by providing free drinking water to those in need. Such compassion shows one's love for his or her neighbor.

However, as we see through the example of the Romans, the convenience of having a clean and sanitary water supply delivered into a home comes with a price. While we have a right to water we have to pay for the resources and the costs that come with such modern conveniences. Furthermore, as I've explained in my past blog post, "Water is not a human right" if we have free water for all, we will bear witness to tragedy of the commons with our water resources.

At a recent symposium on economics and finance, Cardinal Tarcisio Bertone, the Vatican's Secretary of the State, explained the importance of the private sector in water supply. Cardinal Bertone underscores the contribution that the private sector can make to providing access to water. However, he also recognizes the importance that businesses that do provide water are being called to provide an important service to people and morals need to have a higher priority than profit:

> The second challenge has to do with the administration of "common goods" such as water, energy sources, communities, the social and civic capital of peoples and cities. Business today has to become more and more involved with these common goods, since in a complex global economy it can no longer be left to the state or the public sector to administer them: the talent of the business sector is also needed if they are to be properly managed. Where common goods are concerned, we urgently need business leaders for whom profit is not the exclusive goal. More and more, we need business leaders with a social conscience, leaders whose innovation, creativity and efficiency are driven by more than profit, leaders who see their work as part of a new social contract with the public and with civil society.

There is opposition to how water should be supplied. The Catholic left has a different view, supporting government's role in providing water instead of a private entity:

> On June 9, a group of more than 100 missionary priests and nuns fasted and prayed in St. Peter's Square to underline their support for the referendum and their opposition to the privatization of water. Beneath Pope Benedict XVI's windows, they unfurled a giant banner reading: "Lord, help us save the water!"
>
> [...]
>
> Some 25 Italian dioceses signed an appeal asking for a "yes" vote to preserve water as a universally shared resource. Franciscans in Assisi asked prayers and action in defense of "sister water."
>
> Bishop Mariano Crociata, secretary-general of the Italian bishops' conference, said recently that access to clean water

supplies was a "fundamental human right, connected to the very right to life." He warned that privatization efforts have seen multinational companies "turn water into business" to the detriment of the wider population.

And while the U.S. has been criticized for consuming 233 billion gallons of water, it must also be kept in context. The U.S. is still one of the largest and most productive economies, producing goods that are exported to countless countries. Such productivity requires a greater consumption of water than less productive countries, however, every country that does import U.S. goods benefits.

As water is becoming scarcer we will need to reevaluate how we use and treat this precious resource. Yes, we have a obligation to take care of those in need, we must recognize, however the difference between the "right to thirst," to have water in order to sustain life, and the luxury of commoditized water provided through extensive resources to be delivered into homes for domestic use. The Catholic Church teaches that the universal destination of material goods (water is one such good) and the principle of common use of the earth's resources (such as mater) is primarily (though not exclusively) realized the institution of private property—an institution that comes with rights and responsibilities. Applying this reasoning to the dilemmas facing us with regard to water would certainly lead to clearer thinking about this complex question.

"Water—or the lack of it—is one of the biggest issues facing urban Africa."

Water Accessibility Affects All Parts of Society

Moses Mozart Dzawu

In the following viewpoint, author Moses Mozart Dzawu illustrates the water scarcity problem facing the nation of Ghana. By using Ghana as an example, he also offers insight to how water scarcity is negatively affecting African cities in general. One of the most important aspects of the article is the way in which Dzawu shows the real impact of water scarcity on individual, everyday people. He offers details that help explain how water shortages have a domino effect, in that they impact other aspects of life in a nation, such as sanitation, industry, and health. In addition, Dzawu shows the reader how other problems—electricity shortages and population growth—contribute to severe shortages in the availability of safe water. Dzawu is a graduate of the University of Ghana and a reporter at Bloomberg LP.

"A Water Crisis Threatens Ghana's Economic Growth," by Moses Mozart Dzawu, Bloomberg LP, April 12, 2013. Reprinted by permission.

As you read, consider the following questions:

1. What is the severity of the water shortage in Ghana?
2. How does water scarcity impact Ghana's sanitation efforts?
3. How does the electricity crisis make the water scarcity problem more complicated?

Charity Atter's maid, Eva Tetteh, lowers a bucket deep into a well and waits about two minutes for the water to collect inside. Atter, a 37-year-old widow who lives in one of the fast-growing suburbs of Accra, Ghana's capital, has been relying on well water for three years. "The water situation we're facing here is a very difficult problem," she says as she tends customers at her vegetable store in front of her house.

Water—or the lack of it—is one of the biggest issues facing urban Africa, which will see a 66 percent population increase to 1.2 billion people by 2050, according to the United Nations. Although water shortages have long plagued parts of the continent, they've become the potential killer of Africa's economic takeoff. Ghana's $35 billion economy, whose estimated growth of 8 percent in 2013 would outpace the sub-Saharan African average for a sixth straight year, cannot continue at that rate without a modern water network.

Ghana has had peaceful, democratic elections since 1992 and derives its economic strength from gold, cocoa, and oil. Yet in a speech on March 6, Ghanaian President John Dramani Mahama acknowledged that Ghana is "burdened with a major energy and water crisis." The country's network of aging water pipes, some of which date back to 1914, does not reach Accra's expanding and crowded outer suburbs. "Supply cannot meet the increasing demand," says Kweku Botwe, acting managing director of state-owned Ghana Water. "Investment had stagnated so much over the past 40 to 50 years that you're no more dealing with the urgent situation, but with the emergency." Ghana Water can't account for 55 percent of the water it produces, adds Botwe, because Ghanaians illegally siphon water from its pipes, and decrepit pipes damaged by erosion and construction often burst.

The shortage is compounded by a nationwide crisis in electricity production that started when the West African Gas Pipeline broke down last August. That sharply reduced the natural gas available to fire thermal power plants. The water company needs electricity to operate its treatment facilities.

To get water for their operations, companies often pay private water haulers up to 11 times what Ghana Water charges, according to Robert Darko Osei, a research fellow at the University of Ghana's Institute of Statistical, Social and Economic Research. Ayrton Drug Manufacturing bought 12,000 gallons from tanker trucks for 900 cedis ($486) in February, says Chief Accountant Joseph Yaro Abaah. "When water doesn't run for some time, we fall on tanker supplies to feed our factory," he says. Osei says the water crisis is already hurting gross domestic product: With no solution in sight, it's hard to estimate what the ultimate impact will be.

Almost a quarter of greater Accra's population of 4 million doesn't get water from the tap, according to Patrick Apoya, a consultant with the Accra-based Coalition of NGOs in Water and Sanitation. Nationally, that figure is 37 percent. While most Accra neighborhoods hooked up to the utility are supposed to get water pumped into their homes about three times a week, poor infrastructure and unreliable electricity sometimes keep that from happening.

Charity Atter pays a private supplier 35 cedis every three days to fill a water storage tank at her home. It's a backup to the well, which runs low in the dry season. Atter says she pays a shopkeeper 2 cedis a day for purified drinking water. Water delivered to neighborhoods by private operators of tanker-trucks may be contaminated and lead to diseases such as cholera, which killed 31 people in the city last year, says Apoya.

Mohammed Dauda, a driver for a pharmacy in Accra, migrated to the region in 2005 to seek work. The father of six lives in a three-bedroom house without pipe-borne water, he says. He and his family use well water for bathing, washing, and cooking, spending 2 cedis a day on water for drinking, which comes in sealed plastic bags that hold 500 milliliters (0.13 gallons) each. Because they lack water to flush their toilet, Dauda's family uses a public stall, paying 0.80 cedis per use.

"Without a regular flow of water it is difficult to use the water closet; we'd have to buy Poly Tank water at these times that the well is not flowing," says Dauda, 48, using the common brand name for water that comes in plastic containers. "We are not happy with using well water for cooking because you can't guarantee it's kept from pollutants. I wish we had money like the rich to depend solely on Poly Tank water."

The lack of water in Accra affects women and children most, says Ibrahim Musah, the head of policy and partnership at nonprofit WaterAid Ghana. At Nima, Chorkor, and Mamobi, all Accra suburbs where most households are not connected to the utility, the women and children wake up early in the morning because it takes up to an hour to fetch water from a public pipe stand or well. "The children are late for school, and it affects their performance," says Musah. Women, who often prepare food for a living, may struggle to be ready for their customers: "That means her livelihood is affected; if she has children, then there is difficulty looking after them."

Ghana Water is working with foreign investors, including Denys, a Belgian company that's building a €341 million ($438 million) treatment plant, and Befesa Agua, a Spanish-Ghanaian company spending $115 million on a desalination plant. The long-term success of Ghana's economy may depend on these efforts.

> *"Like other crises, the drought offers a view into the institutional and infrastructural relations that are normally not seen, relations that illustrated how the state is bound by political and ecological ties."*

We Must Work Together to Solve Drought Problems

Daniel Polk

One of the most talked-about ecological problems in the United States is the ongoing drought in the state of California. Rather than create divisions in the state, however, Daniel Polk explains in the following viewpoint that Californians understand that every region of their state is being affected by drought and that they must work together. Polk describes the depth of the problem, as well as the various approaches that must be taken to solve it. Polk is an anthropologist at Stanford University, where he researches regional water politics.

As you read, consider the following questions:

1. How has the drought united Californians?
2. What are some of the fears Californians have about the drought and its impact on their lifestyle?
3. In what way does San Diego represent the overall problem with the drought in California?

California is great in size and diversity, the third largest state in the union, with the largest population. The state is comprised of distinct regions and countless enclaves, from Silicon Valley to Los Angeles, from arid basins to frigid peaks, from immense agricultural flatlands to unyielding urban growth. Proposals to split the territory have endured for over a century, often seeking to divide the state between north and south. A recent offer—a failed 2013 ballot petition—would have shattered California into no fewer than six separate states.

The current drought, however, rather than placing strain on lines of division, has resulted in the unchallenged perception of California as one whole. The drought has affected nearly every corner of the state. National and international media portray it as a uniquely California problem, threatening not only "the California lifestyle" but also the state's defining industries of agriculture and suburban growth. California officials have confronted the drought with new state laws and regulations, offering particularly state-bounded solutions. The drought helps to make California appear as a singular object of concern.

The drought highlights how seemingly disparate communities and geographies are connected. And beyond California, people measure lack of rain across the North American West, evident in fallowed fields, reduced fish runs, dried lawns and spreading forest fires. But the drought is not an apocalypse for the West. Although news reports present dire conditions, California will not burst into flames and slide off into the ocean. Difficult decisions, contested calibrations and major shifts in policy are occurring and lie ahead.

Like other crises, the drought offers a view into the institutional and infrastructural relations that are normally not seen, relations that illustrated how the state is bound by political and ecological ties.

One place to explore the drought in California is the coastal city of San Diego. On an average afternoon, downtown can appear ideal, the blue water of the bay and swaying street palms offering a tropical air, with restaurants and hotels catering to the ubiquitous tourist. San Diego is at first glance a place apart. In the southern extremity of California, it is shielded by mountains to the east, a Marine base to the north, the Pacific to the west, and the heavily-guarded U.S./ Mexico border to the south. Historically a rightwing stronghold, San Diego is also a political outlier in a deeply Democratic state. Yet San Diego remains tied to Los Angeles, its northern neighbor, by freeways, railroad and an aqueduct. San Diego leaders have long sought to be free of LA's smog and sprawl, signaling a staunch spirit of civic separateness. Boosters refer to their town as "America's Finest City." But even in idyllic, independent San Diego, the dry spell is a pressing problem.

During field research on California water politics in 2011, I got in touch with a former official who had been among San Diego's leading water managers. I found her office on an upper floor of one of downtown's skyscrapers. The building houses a high-powered legal firm that specializes in water law. Christine Frahm, a senior partner at the firm, served as the Chairwoman of the San Diego County Water Authority from 1997 to 1998.

Reflecting the neoliberal turn in water management a generation ago, Frahm was a leading supporter of a controversial farm-to-city "water transfer." Sometimes referred to as a "water market," the transfer allows San Diego to increase its allocation by drawing water normally used by farmers, who are then economically compensated. The water transfer is a decade-old agreement, linking San Diego's thirst to the abundant supply in the Imperial Valley, a poor farming sector in the desert beyond San Diego.

The water transfer is far from a straight-forward exchange. "In the Imperial Valley, they got their shotguns to defend their water," Frahm said. "It's your life that you're defending." Among Imperial Valley farmers, some are descendants of white settlers who first established water rights a century ago. Often keyed in dramatic terms, water politics thrives on local identities and long-term legacies.

Water's political control rests on a complex of alliances and rivalries that are often unseen by the public. Although federal and state officials oversee policy, water management centers on discreet regional or local districts. From the 19th century to the 21st, water management has ignored popularly-recognized political markers; differences between conservative and liberal, Republican and Democrat, have remained irrelevant to regional histories and insistently local dynamics.

Rather, water politics is defined by distinctions such as agricultural or urban, developers or conservationists, and senior or junior water rights. As scholars Margaret FitzSimmons and Robert Gottlieb have written, California water management can be understood as a kind of "hidden government," whose opaque operations "have rarely stimulated extended controversy or intense debate" [1]. Dictated by insular technical and legal expertise, water management only becomes subject to public scrutiny in times of crisis: floods, legal battles or drought.

The water transfer between San Diego and the Imperial Valley is one such controversy. Prior to the transfer, San Diego relied on Los Angeles for over 90 percent of its water supply. Frahm characterized the water transfer as an attempt to achieve "independence" from LA. Drought in 1992 threatened to cut LA-conveyed water to San Diego by 50 percent. "The '92 drought was the birth of the transfer," Frahm told me.

The present era of water management is defined by increasing reliance on rules, regulations and contracts as well as, to a lesser degree, a free market ideology. Thirty years ago, water managers were usually engineers, "water buffaloes" who lobbied for, built, and maintained vast construction projects. A number of water managers today are not engineers but attorneys. Rather than infrastructural augmentation, reallocation of supply through compacts and regulations lead current strategies to mitigate dwindling sources.

The current drought is part of a long boom-and-bust cycle of downpours and dry spells. Throughout California's history, drought has led to major changes. While drought helps to produce shifts in water usage, drought fundamentally is a political event, determined as much by social practice as by rainfall. The ranching economy of the Spanish and Mexican eras displaced indigenous peoples and flourished until drought struck in the 1860s. It decimated LA and San Diego's thriving cattle industry, transforming the economic landscape more than any drought since. After this, American settlers would establish private water operations here and throughout the West.

By the 20th century, public authorities began to overtake private water companies. Drought became a tool to justify public expansion of infrastructure. Public officials used drought to shore up voter support for the LA Aqueduct in 1905. Drought in the 1930s helped to instigate the building of the Central Valley Project, which supplies part of California's largest agricultural region. Droughts in the 1950s gave pretext to constructing the State Water Project, which spans the spine of California, connecting the wetter north to the arid south. This period was the golden age of Western waterworks, when local, state and federal officials poured countless dollars and labor hours into unprecedented feats of engineering.

This construction boom began to decline by the drought of the 1970s, when neoliberal solutions started displacing an emphasis on infrastructure. Water supplies became tapped to their limit, with few new dams left to build. This led to a focus on efficiency, innovation and market-oriented outcomes. The drought of 1987–92 reinforced this trend, with impact on Southern Californian cities. In years since, the region has launched numerous efforts, with the state's largest desalination plant, water conservation programs, a water-recycling facility, enlarged reservoirs and rural-to-urban water transfers. Today's all-hands approach, based on technologies to extend stressed supplies and regulations to reallocate existing sources, continues to inform how districts battle with drought.

The current drought has entered its fourth year, now one of the driest, warmest periods in recorded state history, hitting hard both farms and cities. Most farming in California occurs in the Central Valley, the 450-mile-long expanse of acreage supplied by the Central Valley Project and State Water Project. These two networks have dramatically cut "ag" water deliveries. To compensate, some farms carry out water transfers, purchasing extra supply from other farms. Also, farmers who can afford it have dug deep wells into dwindling aquifers. This backup supply has allowed the wealthiest farms to hold over, yet groundwater overdraft continues. In some cases, small Central Valley neighborhoods have seen taps run dry. Farmers also have fallowed nearly five percent of Central Valley fields. Poor farmworkers and middle-class farmers struggle while well-capitalized corporate farms are able to more readily absorb the costs of drought.

Agriculture uses approximately 80 percent of water in the state, yet the drought has not significantly affected food prices. Cattle feed including alfalfa, Bermuda grass and Sudan grass use approximately half of the farm water in California. Much of this sustains California's enormous dairy industry; milk and cream are the most lucrative farm commodities. California also exports forage crops to dairies and stockyards in other U.S. states and to countries like China and Japan, fueling a boom in global meat and dairy consumption. California does grow staple crops including rice, corn and wheat, but the state makes more money from cash crops including almonds, grapes and walnuts. California agribusiness serves more to satiate the desires of middle-class tastes than to meet the bare needs of the hungry. Droughts do not imperil the food supply as much as they signal shifts in the costs of producing relatively luxury foods.

Urban water is also constrained, though not with such harsh local impacts as for agriculture. Drinking supplies remain secure for cities. The state has ordered urban districts to practice greater efficiency with a mandate to reduce city water use statewide by 25 percent. The focus of conservation is the semi-tropical foliage adorning much of the state's cityscapes. Approximately 60 percent of urban water goes to landscaping.

The state has long developed with the ideal of lush lawns, towering palm trees and backyard swimming pools. These emblems of California are concentrated in wealthy zip codes, which consume more water than working-class cities. At 145 gallons per day, a resident in Beverly Hills uses 240 percent more water than a resident in Santa Ana, who averages 60 gallons a day. State officials have mandated urban water cuts with these disparities in mind, with wealthier, thirstier jurisdictions called upon to reduce a greater percentage of water usage. Water districts have begun charging tiered water rates, seeking to charge more if citizens use more water.

To meet cuts, water districts are actively promoting alternative landscaping such as drought-resistant plants or artificial lawns. Water districts frequently hold prizes for the most beautiful drought-resistant home gardens. Businesses in Palm Springs advertise services to remove lawns: "When in drought, turf out!" Yard signs in Sacramento proclaim of drying grass, "Gold is the new green." Billboards in San Diego announce, "Let your lawn get a tan." The question for urban water management is not how to quench human thirst, which remains well supplied, but how to articulate a new ethos of water conservation.

From my conversation with Frahm, I better appreciated how representative San Diego's efforts have been. The water transfer marks the unique challenges of combating drought: negotiating new partners, setting new rules and collaborating with state and federal officials. The transfer also mirrors strong environmental concerns that are coupled with water management. The most significant obstacle to the water transfer is environmental impact on the Salton Sea, the largest inland body of water in California, which lies north of the Imperial Valley. Depopulated towns dot the waterfront, appearing as relics of the lake's once-promising former days. Yet for the endangered Yuma Clapper Rail and more than

400 other species of birds, the Salton Sea is a vital haven. Nearly 90 percent of California's wetlands have been lost to development. The Salton Sea remains one of the state's most important wetland habitats for migratory birds, a critical stopover on the Pacific Flyway that extends from Canada to Mexico and further south. The Salton Sea is thus tied to a regional and hemispheric ecology, an often forgotten waterscape closely tied to places far beyond its shores.

In spite of its ecological value, the Salton Sea today appears plagued by constraints. Lying below sea-level in its enclosed basin, it has no ocean outlet, with increasing concentrations of salts, pesticides and fertilizers. Thus the Salton Sea is a highly-saline, eutrophic lake with periodic algae blooms and immense fish "die-offs."

The water transfer will divert farm water that normally drains into the lake. Once the water transfer goes into full effect by 2017 and San Diego begins to receive its full allotment of Imperial irrigation water, local officials anticipate the Salton Sea will irreversibly collapse. Further, its shrinking shoreline will expose fine sediment dust to harsh desert winds, imperiling the air quality and public health of at least one million local residents.

Frahm acknowledged the problem of the Salton Sea, once a side concern that is now a pressing complication. "During negotiations over the water transfer, throughout this whole thing, the Salton Sea has been lurking in the background," she said. The many connections between water management and the environment are well encapsulated in debates around the Salton Sea.

Like other urban officials, Frahm questions the ecological importance of the Salton Sea while recognizing the need to control dust pollution. A solution is required by stipulation of the water transfer agreement. The Imperial Valley and San Diego's water management are thus tied to the fate of the Salton Sea. In the end, Frahm explained, lakebed dust control may be feasible but complete habitat restoration might not be. "In these times," she said, "people have to get realistic about environmental mitigation."

Today's water use regime is inevitably tied to environmental challenges. These challenges are a question not simply of "water resource scarcity" but how to manage the many users of water beyond humans. Simply within California, countless examples proliferate—migratory birds displaced by a dwindling Salton Sea, salmon runs arrested by Klamath River dams or the Bay Delta's fish population threatened by the California Aqueduct. The modern era of water use started with claims to control and reengineer nature. Concerns for environmental consequences helped lead to new scientific disciplines such as ecology, and new governance tools, including environmental impact reports. Diverting water became an exercise in management as well as mitigation.

Drought highlights these underlying conditions of water policy, founded on notions of separation from nature but grounded in close reliance. San Diego's drive for "independence" from LA's water supply has resulted in an intimate reliance on the Imperial Valley's water. The current drought has heightened this dependence, as other sources shrink. With the possibility of more frequent and severe dry spells, the links among institutions, infrastructures and habitats are of growing importance.

Anthropologist Clifford Geertz, writing nearly four decades ago, compellingly addressed modern ecological questions. So-called "natural" systems are inextricably bound with cultural practices, as anthropologists have long shown. Geertz explains, "Though perhaps more apparent in so-called 'traditional' civilizations, this sort of infolding of setting and society is hardly confined to them." He continues:

> It used to be thought that, although environment might shape human life at primitive levels, where men were, it was said, more dependent upon nature, culture-evolutionary advance, especially technical advance, consisted of a progressive freeing of man from such conditioning. But the ecological crisis has divested us all of that illusion; indeed, it may be that advanced technology ties us in even more closely with the habitat we both

make and inhabit, that having more impact upon it we in turn cause it to have more impact upon us. [2]

In relation to climate change, such a viewpoint is more relevant today than ever before. The drought demonstrates how California, a state typically defined as socially fragmented, remains a place woven by political and ecological ties. San Diego exists by virtue of such ties, as efforts to combat drought have linked it more closely with communities such as the Imperial Valley. Even San Diego's wealthy downtown districts remain bound to the fate of the dusty shores of the Salton Sea. Throughout California and beyond its state borders, drought reveals the shared circumstances of disparate people, places, forces and forms of life, bound by both interconnection and interdependence.

Notes

1. Robert Gottlieb and Margaret FitzSimmons. *Thirst for Growth: Water Agencies as Hidden Government in California* (Tucson: University of Ari- zona Press, 1991), xvi–xvii.
2. Clifford Geertz. "The Wet and the Dry: Traditional Irrigation in Bali and Morocco." *Human Ecology* 1, no. 1 (1972): 23–39.

Periodical and Internet Sources Bibliography

The following articles have been selected to supplement the diverse views presented in this chapter.

Kim Bellware, "Global Water Shortage Risk Is Worse Than Scientists Thought," Huffington Post. February 11, 2016. http://www.huffingtonpost.com/entry/water-scarcity-study_us_56c1ebc5e4b0b40245c72f5e

Kate Brauman, "Taking a Closer Look at Global Water Shortages," Smithsonian, June 6, 2016. http://www.smithsonianmag.com/science-nature/global-water-shortages-180959318/#bWeOrXT7Va4RTX0p.99

CDC: Centers for Disease Control and Prevention, "Global Water, Sanitation, & Hygiene (WASH)." https://www.cdc.gov/healthywater/global/wash_statistics.html

Robin McKie, "Why Fresh Water Shortages Will Cause the Next Great Global Crisis," The Guardian, March 7, 2015. https://www.theguardian.com/environment/2015/mar/08/how-water-shortages-lead-food-crises-conflicts

National Geographic, "Freshwater Crisis." http://environment.nationalgeographic.com/environment/freshwater/freshwater-crisis/

Jon Neale and Jonathan Thompson, "Eau, No: Clean, Healthy and Pure? Hardly," The Independent, February 12, 2006. http://www.independent.co.uk/environment/eau-no-clean-healthy-and-pure-hardly-bottled-water-is-killing-the-planet-6109336.html

Seametrics, "25 Facts You Should Know About the Global Water Crisis," September 15, 2014. http://www.seametrics.com/blog/global-water-crisis-facts/

Shannyn Snyder, "Waste Water Pathogens," The Water Project. https://thewaterproject.org/Wastewater%20Pathogens.pdf

The Water Project, "Bottled Water is Wasteful." https://thewaterproject.org/bottled-water/bottled_water_wasteful

World Water Council, "Water: The Key for Global Development." 2013. http://www.worldwatercouncil.org/fileadmin/world_water_council/documents/official_documents/WWC_2013AnnualReport.pdf

OPPOSING
VIEWPOINTS®
SERIES

CHAPTER 2

What Is Causing
Water Scarcity?

Chapter Preface

There is no doubt that safe water is becoming more scarce—it's the reasons why that are being debated.

For example, some experts claim that the reason is due to simple numbers: Earth's human population has never been this high. Currently, there are over 7 billion people on our planet, all of whom require water to live, to grow their food, to maintain hygiene, and for other purposes. The population boom in recent years is putting extra stress on the planet and straining its resources.

Others argue that the human population is affecting the earth's water supply not in terms of its growing numbers, but because of the damage humans are causing to the environment. Scientists have been issuing warnings for decades that the environment is being damaged and the Earth is at risk. Human behavior has been modified; in the last fifteen years, for example, recycling has become a routine habit for many Americans. But more needs to be done, because the safety of our water is also at risk.

Climate change is real, and global warming is being intensified due to human causes, primarily greenhouse gases. Our industries and transportation systems are allowing gases—especially carbon dioxide, methane, nitrous oxide, and water vapor—to enter the atmosphere. These gas emissions are rising to levels that are quite high. The accumulation of gases in the atmosphere is making the earth hotter, which is causing extreme droughts and floods.

Still others see the chief problem in mismanagement: humans are notoriously wasteful and do not handle water distribution in ways that are fair and sustainable. For example, power plants, factory farms, and other industries require massive amounts of water to operate, which is draining water reserves. In China, for example, the industrial complex has been blamed for putting an undue strain on water resources. Humans waste water on an individual level as well: many homes have vast landscaping designs that require regular watering, which is wasteful because the water is not being used for consumption but for aesthetic purposes. In American states where drought has crippled the economy and local population, watering one's lawn and filling one's swimming pool with water have become frowned-upon or even illegal practices.

Is it population growth or global warming, waste and mismanagement, or something else entirely? This chapter offers myriad points of view on the reasons why our planet is running out of safe water.

> *"The average fracking well uses between 2.5 million and 5 million gallons of freshwater, seven times as much as the exploration of traditional natural gas."*

Fracking Contributes to Water Scarcity

Joshua Pringle

In the following viewpoint, Joshua Pringle argues that the process of hydraulic fracturing, or fracking, is a leading cause of water scarcity. First, he explains the ways in which fracking damages the environment (for example, it not only contaminates local water sources, but it can also trigger earthquakes), and then he offers information on how much water is wasted in the fracking process. For example, he reports that a fracking well consumes 2.5 to 5 million gallons of freshwater, significantly more than the amount used by traditional methods of accessing natural gas. Using examples from China and the United States, Pringle argues that fracking is a worldwide problem that should be stopped. Pringle has a master's in international relations from New York University. He is the senior editor of Worldpress.org.

As you read, consider the following questions:

1. How do fracking wells and methods damage the local environment?
2. How do politicians and government agencies contribute to the problem?
3. How does fracking lead to water waste and scarcity?

F or this year's World Water Day, the United Nations focused on the relationship between water and energy. Energy is an unavoidable necessity, but energy production uses enormous amounts of water. Consequently, as global energy demands increase, water scarcity grows more acute. According to the U.N. report, "Currently, 90 percent of energy production relies on intensive and non-reusable water models that are not sustainable." The climate-change loop only exacerbates this problem. As more fossil fuels are burned, more greenhouse gases are released into the atmosphere, warming the planet and increasing the frequency and severity of droughts.

The U.N. report projects that global water demand will increase by 55 percent by mid-century, and that more than 40 percent of the world's population will be living in areas of extreme water stress. Water scarcity is most critical in developing parts of Africa and Asia, where scarcity threatens human needs as well as agriculture, industry and the potential for economic growth. But water problems are hardly exclusive to developing countries. The latest U.S. Drought Monitor shows that 38 percent of the continental United States is experiencing moderate to exceptional drought (almost all of it west of the Mississippi River). California—which produces nearly half of the country's fruits, vegetables and nuts—is in its third year of drought, with water reserves this year on track to be the worst in 500 years.

California also sits on the Monterey Shale formation, which holds more shale oil than anywhere else in the country, and which has oil companies drooling over the fracking possibilities. Fracking, however, threatens water supplies in a number of ways, putting the tension between water and energy into sharp relief. There is a similar tension in parts of northern China, where water scarcity is alarming, and yet where the government is incentivizing companies to frack for natural gas. As the U.N. Intergovernmental Panel on Climate Change warns the world yet again that we really need to take serious steps to address climate change in the next few years, extreme methods of energy extraction warrant serious consideration of the irreversible damage those methods wreak.

Hydraulic Fracturing

Fracking involves blasting water mixed with chemicals and sand into rock formations buried deep in the earth in order to extract oil and gas. About 25 percent of those chemicals are carcinogens. When cement casings crack and leak, the chemicals contaminate groundwater, turning water supplies toxic, rendering properties worthless, poisoning wildlife. Fracking also releases hazardous gases like methane and benzene into the atmosphere, poisoning the air. Methane is an exponentially more potent greenhouse gas than carbon dioxide—gasoline on the fire for climate change. And according to a study in the Proceedings of the National Academy of the Sciences, fracking sites in Pennsylvania's Marcellus Shale, which is rich in natural gas, are releasing between 100 and 1,000 times as much methane as EPA estimates. Plus, fracking induces earthquakes. So when U.S. President Barack Obama touts natural gas as a bridge to a clean energy future, there's plenty he's not mentioning.

On top of all that, the average fracking well uses between 2.5 million and 5 million gallons of freshwater, seven times as much as the exploration of traditional natural gas. For Californians near the Monterey Shale, this is particularly distressing. "California is in the midst of a historic drought, and fracking exacerbates that," Kassie Siegel, director of the Center for Biological Diversity's Climate Law Institute, tells *Worldpress.org*. "Fracking uses enormous quantities of fresh water, and once you use that water it's contaminated and is removed from the water cycle for good."

The Center for Biological Diversity is among more than 150 organizations that have joined the Californians Against Fracking coalition, which is calling on Governor Jerry Brown to ban fracking. "The vision of the majority of Californians is that fracking has no place in our state," Siegel says. "The oil companies are the only ones that are going to benefit from the fracking boom in California. ... In fact, renewable energy is far better for California's economy. Investing in renewable energy creates far more jobs than investing in further fossil fuel development." There is movement on the issue. A bill in the California Senate to place a moratorium on fracking has passed its first committee and will be heard by a second committee in a week. Meanwhile, cities in California like Santa Cruz and Carson have passed their own moratoriums.

China

The United States is way out in front of any other country on the fracking boom. In the Eagle Ford Shale area in Texas alone, more than 8,000 oil and gas wells are actively drilling, with another 5,000 in the pipeline. There are about 40,000 in the country overall. China has fewer than 100. Although, China is looking to make up that ground, with a target of producing 6.5 billion cubic meters of shale next year and 60 billion to 100 billion cubic meters by 2020. Those are aggressive growth projections, but China's Ministry of Land and Resources estimates that the country's shale gas reserves are the biggest in the world, a third larger than those in the United States.

Last month, state oil and gas company Sinopec announced significant breakthroughs at a fracking site in the south of China. In response, the government raised the prices paid for new gas supply and made natural gas pipelines open to third-party drillers, thus further opening up the gas market. But again, much of China's climate is extremely arid. According to the Scholars Strategy Network, "Few places in the world are facing such acute scarcity of water as is northern China, the region surrounding the nation's capital in Beijing. Over the past three decades, rapid economic development and population growth have caused a dramatic water shortage in the region. Groundwater tables have dropped so precipitously that in some places wells cannot be dug deep enough to reach water." China has launched two massive, complicated national projects to address water scarcity, but "if they fail or fall apart, as seems likely, these efforts could actually make water scarcity much worse."

Long-term versus Short-term Thinking

China has to find a way to meet its ballooning energy needs, but at what cost? All of North America should be asking the same question, as debates are happening right now in Mexico and Canada as well. Murmurs can even be heard about fracking in Europe now that the showdown with Russia has everyone sweating. There are multiple reasons to oppose fracking, but the water issue has to be at the top of the list. No one wants to live without sufficient energy supplies, but living without sufficient water isn't possible. As climate change deepens the problem, developed and developing countries alike need leadership that is geared toward the long term. (For an example of complete wrongheadedness on the water issue, see the World Bank's plans for water privatization.)

In the United States, the EPA has totally dropped the ball on fracking, especially with regard to water contamination. Cowing to political pressure, the agency closed investigations into contamination in Wyoming, Pennsylvania and Texas in 2012 and 2013. An EPA document leaked last year showed that fracking had indeed contaminated aquifers in Pennsylvania, contrary to the agency's official position. Also last year, the investigation in Wyoming was essentially turned over to the drilling company that owned the wells in question.

From the bottom up, though, people are being activated on the fracking issue every day, because it affects them where they live. As the dangers of fracking become increasingly apparent, voices in opposition grow louder and more numerous. And just yesterday, a jury in Texas awarded a family $3 million in its suit against a fracking company. The family sued because the company exposed them to hazardous gases and made them sick. A judge still has to sign off, and appeals may follow, but it's a blow against the industry, one sure to be lauded by citizens from California to New York. After all, this boom is making plenty of people sick.

> *"It's not accurate to claim that climate change is at the root of growing water scarcity around the world."*

To Solve Water Scarcity, Slow the Human Population Growth

Robert Engelman

In the following viewpoint, Robert Engelman rejects the idea that water scarcity is most impacted by climate change. There is another factor involved in water scarcity, he suggests, one that is easier to fix— the growth in the human population. In researching the many articles that relate to water scarcity, Engelman concluded that the problem would be more affected by slowing down the population boom. The link is clear: a lower birth rate would mean less people putting a burden on the freshwater supply of the planet. More control of family planning would also help improve the lives of women around the world, Engleman adds. Engleman is a senior fellow at the Worldwatch Institute, project director of the Family Planning and Environmental Sustainability Assessment, and lead author of "Family Planning and Environmental Sustainability: Assessing the Science."

"When It Comes to Water Scarcity, Population Growth Tops Climate Change," by Robert Engelman, Environmental Change and Security Program, August 1, 2016. Reprinted by permission.

As you read, consider the following questions:

1. How does the author determine that the real problem is population growth, not climate change?
2. In which ways can population growth be slowed?
3. What are the other positive benefits of reducing population growth?

One of the findings of the Worldwatch Institute's Family Planning and Environmental Sustainability Assessment (FPESA) suggests it's not accurate to claim that climate change is at the root of growing water scarcity around the world. Based on the best recent scientific evidence we could find, another major global trend—the ongoing growth of human population—has a greater impact on water availability than climate change does.

On June 29 at the Wilson Center, FPESA released a report of findings after more than two years of collaboratively assessing more than 900 peer-reviewed scientific papers published in the last 12 years on the relationship between family planning, population, and the environment. The balance of the evidence falls short of scientific confirmation of our main hypothesis, that investments in family planning directly promote environmental sustainability. But the evidence assembled nonetheless offers strong support for the idea. Many studies point to related but less comprehensive conclusions about the value of family planning in the context of the environment and next to none offer evidence that family planning is environmentally irrelevant or harmful.

Among our core conclusions is that the use of family planning clearly helps women and couples prevent unwanted pregnancy. This reduces fertility, raises the average age of childbearing, and slows population growth. Slower population growth translates into a slower accumulation of environmental pressures stemming from human activity. Even apart from its demographic influence on the environment, the use of family planning appears to contribute to the empowerment of women. This, in turn, helps women

The Impact of Climate Change on Water Resources

As the earth's temperature continues to rise, we can expect a significant impact on our fresh water supplies with the potential for devastating effects on these resources. As temperatures increase, evaporation increases, sometimes resulting in droughts. The US is currently in one of the most severe, multi-state, multi-year droughts in decades.

In addition, rising temperatures are melting glacial ice at an unprecedented rate. Glaciers are an important source of freshwater worldwide, and some, like those at Glacier National Park, are in danger of disappearing within the 21st century. Once these glaciers have melted away, they can't be restored. Areas that previously depended on glaciers for freshwater will then have to seek other sources.

Complicating this potential outcome is the prediction that in a warmer environment, more precipitation will occur as rain rather than snow. Although more rain than snow may seem like a plus, it could mean more frequent water shortages. When snow and ice collect on mountaintops, water is released slowly into reservoirs as it melts throughout the spring and summer. When rain falls, reservoirs fill quickly to capacity in the winter, which can also result in excess water runoff that can't be stored. Because rain flows faster than melting snow, higher levels of soil moisture and groundwater recharge are less likely to occur. Areas that rely on snowmelt as their primary freshwater source could increasingly experience water shortages, like having low water supplies by summer's end.

Conserving water, food and other resources is an important step towards reducing overall energy use, because most everything that is made, transported and thrown away requires the use of fuel and water. By carpooling, using public transportation, driving less, and reducing our consumption of food and consumer goods, each individual can make an impact on curbing greenhouse gases.

"The Impact of Climate Change on Water Resources," GRACE Communications Foundation.

take more active civic and economic roles, which contributes to environmental sustainability.

One finding that stood out was a group of papers that considered an intriguing question: Which has more impact on present or future water scarcity, climate change or population growth? Put another way, if population growth proceeded in the absence of climate change, or if climate change proceeded in the absence of population growth, which would be worse for the availability of freshwater?

Doing the Math

Put simply, not a single paper that we could identify found climate change to have a greater impact than population growth on water availability. Most found population growth the stronger force, though a few simply treated both forces as major threats to water availability without concluding which was more important. A few papers found growth in human demand—related to population but certainly not limited to it—to matter more than decreases in water supply due to climate change.

These findings are logically unsurprising, despite being missed by many commentators. Though often renewable, freshwater is a finite natural resource essential to life. As former Vice President Al Gore used to note, there's no more of it today than when Moses was in the bulrushes. And human beings cannot survive without minimal amounts of water.

In the 1990s, Swedish hydrologist Malin Falkenmark developed categories of water stress and scarcity based on annual per capita needs at various stages of economic development. These could be calculated easily by comparing available renewable freshwater with watershed populations. Applying these benchmarks of water stress and scarcity, it's easy to see how powerful a force population growth can be. Twice as many people in a watershed means half as much of the water available to each person. (Problems of access then complicate matters more, but they must contend with the basic equation of availability.)

Climate change, by contrast, may increase or decrease the supply of water, depending on a complex mix of precipitation trends and the greater evaporation caused by warmer temperatures. The actual impact on available water is hard to predict, and projections of impacts on the hydrologic cycle are often diverse for a single watershed or region.

In the last few decades, meanwhile, population growth in many or even most water basins has been more dramatic than any changes in climate. Demographers project future population growth, based on the population momentum propelled by young people already born and the slowness of changes in fertility, with more confidence than climate change experts project how precipitation will change with rising temperatures.

The peer-reviewed papers the FPESA project surveyed bore this logic out.

Robert I. McDonald and colleagues concluded that by 2050 population growth in cities in the developing world will multiply the number of people perennially short of water seven-fold, from 150 million to 1 billion. Projected climate change, they found, will add 100 million people to this number—no trivial growth increment, but still a much smaller one.

Another study we annotated and assessed, by Richard C. Carter and Alison Parker, projected that the combined force of population growth and urbanization in Africa will "dwarf the likely impacts of climate change on groundwater resources, at least in the first half of the 21st century."

Yongbo Liu and Yaning Chen performed a calculation that we felt could probably be performed in many watersheds to compare the relative impacts of climate change and, if not population growth per se, at least changing human demand for water. They compared changes in stream flow of the headwaters of the Tarim River in Western China with changes in downstream flow where human populations were withdrawing this water. While water was less available to people downstream, there was actually more of it upstream over the last three decades—a clear indication that, at least in this case, it was demand for water rather than overall supply decreases that caused scarcity.

Not Every Problem Is a Climate Problem

Do these papers—and more we identified drawing this conclusion— prove beyond a doubt that population growth matters more to water scarcity or other environmental problems than climate change? Not hardly. Science is, after all, an iterative process, advancing over time toward what is real and true but never actually reaching the finish line.

But the absence of papers calculating greater effects from climate change on water supply is at least telling, especially when combined with the logic of how rising human demand interacts with changing supplies of a resource.

Of course, we can't say for sure we caught every single paper related to the linkage we were studying (though we believe we found most in the time period examined). What we can say is that the FPESA project identified a tendency among researchers in recent peer-reviewed literature to conclude that current or projected population growth is a stronger or more certain driver of some specific environmental problems, especially water scarcity, than current or projected climate change.

There are communications and policy implications in this finding. Scientists, experts, and journalists should more often explore the power of population growth in placing demands on finite supplies of freshwater rather than reflexively pointing the finger at climate change. An example of a commentary acknowledging the combined impacts of both population growth and climate change on water, but then focusing solely on climate change, can be seen in this Washington Post editorial from last May.

While neither population growth nor climate change are amenable to easy solutions or swift turnarounds, there are logical ways to address each, compatible with the values of human rights and reducing inequality. Since the widespread use of contraception yields slower population growth, among its many other benefits, and since continued population growth today is very likely a factor in environmental decline, encouraging access to and the use of voluntary family planning is likely to have environmental benefits—not the least of which is more freshwater availability.

> *"Urban subsidence is a type of geological disaster, and it's a problem for all cities worldwide because of the excessive extraction of groundwater."*

Water Scarcity Is Caused by Excessive Extraction of Groundwater

Feng Hao

In the following viewpoint, Feng Hao argues that many of the world's busiest, most populated cities are sinking—yes, sinking. Hao offers an overview of the problem, and then provides an informational interview with Long Di, a professor at Tsinghua University's Institute of Hydrology and Water Resources in Beijing, China. There are two reasons, according to the authors: the growing urban population, and also the increasing rate of subsidence, which is the process of extracting fresh water from underground. As water is extracted, perhaps at higher levels than the earth can sustain, gaps are created in rock layers, which may collapse - thus causing the ground itself to sink. According to Long Di, subsidence is not a reversible process. Feng Hao is a researcher at chinadialogue.

As you read, consider the following questions:

1. Which cities are most affected by subsidence?
2. What is subsidence and how does it lead to sinking?
3. Why are governments allowing overdrafting of groundwater?

In China's arid north, the natural water supply fails to meet the needs of many cities. In Beijing, the country's capital, water is pumped up from millennia-old aquifers that lie deep underground. But over-extraction of water in this region has shrunk a dwindling resource and subsidence is now an urgent problem, especially for the residents of Beijing whose water needs are growing fastest.

Subsidence is caused by the degradation of permeable rock hundreds of feet underground. When water is pumped up from this rock to the surface, it leaves behind pockets of air that eventually collapse causing the land and the cities built above it to "sink".

In June, a Chinese-led study revealed that Beijing is dropping by 11 centimetres per year. The research, published in the peer-reviewed journal *Remote Sensing*, was based on a type of radar that records land elevation changes called InSAR.

But in Beijing people care little for the loss of water beneath them, focusing more on the air pollution above ground. Long Di, a professor at Tsinghua University's Institute of Hydrology and Water Resources in Beijing told *chinadialogue* that it is time to pay attention.

Long Di (LD): There are two contexts to consider. One is the global process of urbanisation; the other is loss of groundwater on China's northern plains. Urban subsidence is a type of geological disaster, and it's a problem for all cities worldwide because of the excessive extraction of groundwater. Tokyo has already sunk by two metres. Central Valley in California, Venice, Bangkok, Ho Chi Minh, Jakarta – all these cities are suffering or have suffered from subsidence. But the northern plains of China are one of the worst affected areas worldwide due to the degree of extraction.

Three decades of rapid economic development, urbanisation and large-scale irrigation, interspersed with climate extremes (for example, drought) has increased the demand on groundwater supplies.

Our joint research team, with associate professor Pan Yun of Capital Normal University, analysed data from 131 monitoring wells on China's northern plains from 2005 to 2013. It found that the incidence and the depth of subsidence were increasing, most notably in the Shijiazhuang-Tianjin-Beijing region.

CD: What effect is subsidence having on the lives of ordinary people in Beijing? Should they be worried?

LD: Subsidence is a slow but progressive disaster, and it is irreversible. It can cause cracks in walls, roads, bridges, and underground municipal infrastructure, such as subway tunnels. In cases of serious damage the only option may be to demolish and rebuild, which is particularly bad for areas under historical or cultural protection. It can also affect the course of rivers, leading to flooding.

Monitoring by the geological authorities has found the worst subsidence in Tianjin, north of Beijing, where land has dropped by 3.6 metres in total.

Subsidence also severs links between groundwater and surface water features such as rivers and lakes, which are more likely to dry up as groundwater stops feeding in. Coastal areas may have to deal with an ingress of saltwater. This can be disastrous for ecosystems.

CD: What is that state of Beijing's groundwater?

LD: The situation is quite grave. Figures from the Beijing Water Authority show that the groundwater level fell 9 metres between 2000 and 2011, an average of 60 to 75 centimetres a year. In early 2005, the groundwater depth was 20 metres, by the end of 2011 it had fallen to 24.7 metres; an average drop of 70 centimetres a year. But since 2011 this has slowed to 30 centimetres a year.

Both manmade and natural events have played a role. Beijing saw more precipitation between 2011 and 2013, which aided a rapid recovery of shallow groundwater resources. Meanwhile,

DROUGHT AND CLIMATE CHANGE

Drought ranks second in terms of national weather-related economic impacts, with annual losses nearing $9 billion per year in the U.S. Beyond direct economic impacts, drought can threaten drinking water supplies and ecosystems, and can even contribute to increased food prices.

Within the last decade, drought conditions have hit the Southeastern U.S., the Midwest, and the Western U.S. In 2011, Texas had the driest year since 1895. In 2013, California had the driest year on record.

When considering the relationship of drought to climate change, it is important to make the distinction between weather and climate. Weather is a description of atmospheric conditions over a short period of time, while climate is how the atmosphere behaves over relatively long periods of time.

Individual drought periods can be understood as discrete weather events. Climate changes occur over longer periods and can be observed as changes in the patterns of weather events. For instance, as temperatures have warmed over the past century, the prevalence and duration of drought has increased in the American West.

Global climate change affects a variety of factors associated with drought. There is high confidence that increased temperatures will lead to more precipitation falling as rain rather than snow, earlier snow melt, and increased evaporation and transpiration. Thus the risk of hydrological and agricultural drought increases as temperatures rise.

Much of the Mountain West has experienced declines in spring snowpack, especially since mid-century. These declines are related to a reduction in precipitation falling as snow (with more falling as rain), and a shift in timing of snowmelt. Earlier snowmelt, associated with warmer temperatures, can lead to water supply being increasingly out of phase with water demands.

While there is some variability in the models for western North America as a whole, climate models unanimously project increased drought in the American Southwest. The Southwest is considered one of the more sensitive regions in the world for increased risk of drought caused by climate change.

"Causes of Drought: What's the Climate Connection?" Union of Concerned Scientists.

construction of the South-North Water Transfer Project [China's largest ever water diversion project, which redirects water from China's southern rivers to northern areas], has reduced demands on groundwater in the northeast.

CD: How much of Beijing's groundwater shortage is due to the "historical debt" accrued from years of over-extraction of groundwater?

LD: Beijing has per capita water resources of less than 100 cubic metres, one twentieth of the national average and one eightieth of the global, and far off an internationally recognised danger level of 1,700 cubic metres. According to the municipal Water Authority, Beijing used an average of 3.5 billion cubic metres of water a year between 2006 and 2011—with under 2.5 billion cubic metres of that usually coming from renewable water sources. Before the North-South Water Transfer Project the gap had to be made up by groundwater extraction, hence the long-term drain on those reserves.

CD: The water authority's figures show that in 2015 groundwater levels in the city increased for the first time in 16 years. What was the role of the water transfer project in that?

LD: The data show that as of May 9, the first stage of the North-South Water Transfer Project's central route had provided more than 1.2 billion cubic metres of water to the capital.

Since water started flowing into Beijing along this route in December 2014, drecreases in groundwater levels have slowed significantly. With precipitation in 2014 being 60 centimetres less than the multiyear average and no increase in precipitation in 2015, data from the GRACE satellite monitoring shows that the city's total water reserves remained stable, and even saw some recovery in early 2016.

CD: The water transfer project has been controversial for its high cost, environmental impact and massive displacement of local population. What's your view?

LD: The population is increasing and becoming more concentrated, urbanisation is still underway, this has created a water gap, and so what do we do? In the past we extracted groundwater. But if we want to slow manmade subsidence we have to slow or even stop groundwater extraction. It's not like air pollution—deep groundwater aquifers take thousands or tens of thousands of years to form. It's like oil—every drop you use is a drop lost, it's not renewable.

In the short-term, further rollout of the project [which by 2030 is set to bring 1.8-2 billion cubic metres of water to Beijing every year] and changes to our industrial structure give hope that loss of groundwater and related issues such as subsidence and salt-water incursion will be resolved to varying degrees.

CD: Apart from water transfer projects, what else can be done to reduce groundwater use in Beijing?

LD: There's a range of things that can be done. Either increasing surface water availability or reducing demand for groundwater. Increasing surface water availability could include making more space to store urban rainwater, so that it can be collected and used. Reducing demand for groundwater could mean reducing agriculture, which uses groundwater for irrigation, or increasing its water efficiency.

Making withdrawals from aquifers only during dry periods of water stored in normal times would be a sustainable way of managing groundwater. Improving the industrial structure, cutting back in water-intensive sectors, raising awareness of water conservation among residents—these are all key to reducing overuse of groundwater and achieving sustainable use.

"The impacts of groundwater overdraft are numerous, complex, costly, and have a reach that extends far beyond groundwater pumpers."

Groundwater Overdrafting Must be Regulated

Tara Moran, Janny Choy, and Carolina Sanchez

In the following viewpoint, Tara Moran, Janny Choy, and Carolina Sanchez argue that groundwater overdrafting is causing permanent damage to the environment, as well as a degraded quality of water. There is also a higher level of energy usage, as water has to be pumped at deeper levels because of groundwater depletion. Groundwater reserves may be able to replenish and recover, the authors contend, but legislation needs to regulate the overdrafting before more permanent damage is caused. The authors prepared this report for Stanford University's Water in the West program, which is meant to help people understand groundwater resources in order to better utilize them. Moran is Program Lead, Sustainable Groundwater for Stanford's Water in West Sustainable Groundwater Program. Choy is a California and Western Water Policy Specialist. Sanchez is a staff engineer at Wildermuth Environmental.

As you read, consider the following questions:

1. What are the various negative effects of groundwater overdrafting?
2. How can groundwater drafting be managed or regulated more effectively?
3. What is subsidence and how can it damage the environment?

G roundwater overdraft occurs when groundwater use exceeds the amount of recharge into an aquifer, which leads to a decline in groundwater level. This condition is occurring in an increasing number of groundwater basins throughout California, and is impacting the state in many ways.

The Effects of Groundwater Overdraft

Direct impacts of groundwater overdraft include reduced water supply due to aquifer depletion or groundwater contamination, increased groundwater pumping costs, and the costs of well replacement or deepening. An increasing number of people with domestic wells are seeing them dry up, leading to conflicts. Rural landowners and small-scale farmers are disproportionately affected by overdraft as they have fewer financial resources to dig new or deeper wells or diversify their water supply.

Less obvious are the indirect consequences of groundwater overdraft, which include land subsidence and infrastructure damage, harm to groundwater-dependent ecosystems, and the economic losses from a more unreliable water supply for California.

Many of these impacts are not exclusive to groundwater overdraft. But overdraft will generally exacerbate pre-existing conditions or create new ones entirely.

Land Subsidence is Not Just an Artifact of the Past

When large volumes of water are removed from a groundwater basin, compaction of the aquifers can occur as clay layers are drained, causing land subsidence—an actual drop in the land's elevation. Most subsidence is inelastic, meaning that the land surface will not rebound even if previous groundwater levels are restored. Preventing subsidence is therefore vital.

Land surface elevation changes can have serious consequences for infrastructure, including the loss of conveyance capacity in canals, diminished levee effectiveness, and damage to roads, bridges, building foundations, and pipelines. It can also lead to the development of earth fissures, which can damage surface and subsurface structures, as well as provide pathways for contaminants to enter shallow aquifers.

Some areas of the state that have experienced subsidence resulting from groundwater overdraft have stabilized groundwater elevations through good management. For example, portions of the land surface of the Santa Clara Valley subsided approximately 13 feet in the first half of the 20th century. Since then, the Santa Clara Valley Water District has successfully halted additional subsidence by recharging groundwater, diversifying its water supply to include surface water, regulating groundwater withdrawals, and implementing a monitoring program.

A Sinking Feeling in San Jose

While some basins have made good progress, subsidence continues today in many parts of the state, sometimes at a rate of more than 1 foot/year. In the San Joaquin Valley, subsidence from groundwater extraction has greatly impacted infrastructure such as the San Joaquin River, Delta Mendota Canal, Friant-Kern Canal and San Luis Canal, as well as private canals, bridges, pipelines, and storm sewers.

Technological advances have made monitoring of land subsidence more accurate. Interferometric Synthetic Aperture Radar (InSAR), which provides accurate measures of changes in the land surface elevation, has been used to monitor land subsidence in California's Central Valley. New research from Stanford University is expanding the capabilities of this tool: a study of Colorado's San Luis Valley correlated changes in land deformation with estimates of changing groundwater elevations, effectively allowing the measurement of groundwater levels across large areas by satellite.

Energy Needs Ramp Up as Groundwater Goes Down

It takes a great deal of energy to heat, treat, and move water. This is particularly true in California, where water-related electricity use accounts for nearly 20% of California's total electricity consumption. The State Water Project, for example, uses a great deal of energy to move water more than 700 miles and nearly 2000 feet up and over the Tehachapi Mountains from Northern to Southern California.

Energy demand from groundwater use is less apparent, but the total energy required to pump groundwater from thousands of individual groundwater wells across the state—estimated at 6000 gigawatt hours—is higher than the annual energy requirements for the entire State Water Project.

Reliance on groundwater for irrigation and a growing population have lead to greater groundwater use and chronically declining groundwater elevations in many parts of the state. Many areas of the San Joaquin Valley are experiencing groundwater levels more than 100 feet below previous historical lows, as chronic groundwater elevation declines are exacerbated by the current drought. This has important implications for energy use and greenhouse gas emissions, as more energy is needed to pump the groundwater up from those greater depths.

Additionally, the majority of agricultural groundwater pumping happens during the summer, which coincides with peak energy demand in California. This is enormously taxing on the state's electrical grid. The California Public Utilities Commission estimates that electricity used for groundwater pumping during summer months exceeds that used for pumping the State Water Project, Central Valley Project, and Colorado River Aqueduct combined.

Cities and domestic well users are also suffering from declining groundwater elevations. Fresno, which gets approximately 85% of its water supply from groundwater, withdraws about twice as much water from its aquifer as is recharged by rainfall and stream flows each year. Even with some artificial recharge, groundwater elevations have continued to decline. As a result, the city is struggling with increased electricity costs associated with pumping deeper groundwater, as well as the cost of deepening existing wells and the need for new wells.

Some agencies are taking steps to better understand the energy requirements of their water system before problems occur. The Regional Water Authority, which helps local water agencies in the greater Sacramento region plan for effective conjunctive use management programs, is working with the Sacramento Municipal Utility District (SMUD) to develop a baseline understanding of the energy intensity of the different components of their water system, including groundwater. The primary goal of the SMUD-funded study is to identify improvements that will reduce both water and energy demands, thus reducing greenhouse gas emissions. With this information they can better manage peak energy demand and energy-related expenses, particularly during dry conditions when the more energy-intensive groundwater becomes the dominant source of water supply.

Water Quality Problems Can Be Amplified by Groundwater Overdraft

Groundwater overdraft can create new water quality problems or make existing groundwater pollution worse. As aquifer levels decline from chronic overdraft, natural and manmade pollutants can concentrate in the remaining groundwater, making it unsafe for irrigation or drinking without costly treatment. In some cases, wells must be shut down.

All groundwater contains some dissolved minerals derived from the local geology. In addition to naturally-occurring salts and minerals, manmade pollutants such as nitrates, petroleum products, and synthetic chemicals can get into groundwater basins from agricultural and dairy operations, industrial plants, unlined landfills, septic systems, military bases and other sources.

- **Fertilizers and pesticides** from agricultural fields and feedlots get into aquifers and concentrate in heavily pumped groundwater aquifers. High nitrate levels are a widespread problem in agricultural regions of California, affecting the water supply for many communities in the Central Valley and Central Coast. In many cases, direct remediation to remove nitrate from large groundwater basins is extremely costly and not technically feasible. As a result, many communities have had to seek supplemental water supplies. Groundwater recharge is the most common solution for nitrate contaminated aquifers.
- **Salts from various sources** can accumulate in groundwater, threatening drinking water and agricultural supplies. For example, the cities of Davis and Woodland, formerly 100% dependent on groundwater, are diversifying their water supply portfolio to include some surface water because salt accumulation in groundwater as well as disposal of salt-laden wastewaters after human use is becoming a problem.
- **Saltwater intrusion** can occur in coastal groundwater basins, where overpumping of groundwater aquifers can cause seawater to be drawn into aquifers and contaminate the water supply. Changing groundwater management practices and the creation of a freshwater "wall" through injection wells are the most common solutions for saltwater intrusion.
- **Industrial pollutants** come from a variety of sources and can enter groundwater aquifers through land surface spills or contaminated surface water sources. In the San Fernando Basin in Southern California, groundwater contamination from industrial pollutants has forced the Los Angeles

Department of Power and Water to shut down about half of their water wells in the basin. The city is planning to spend approximately $700 million to treat contaminated groundwater in the San Fernando Basin to make the water usable again.

Groundwater contamination is often costly to remediate; prevention is therefore the key. To keep groundwater supplies clean and safe, some required actions include sustaining groundwater elevations over time, regulating pollutant discharges to surface and groundwater, and a thoughtful consideration of appropriate land uses in recharge areas.

The Steep Price of Overpumping for Many Ecosystems

Groundwater and surface water are connected in a variety of ways. Many rivers, streams, wetlands, springs, lakes, and terrestrial vegetation—and the wildlife they support—are dependent on groundwater. Conflicts between groundwater use and these groundwater-dependent ecosystems in California have recently been mapped and summarized in this series. Conflicts from groundwater pumping have occurred over solar power plants, fish hatcheries, gravel mines, groundwater substitution transfers and other activities.

For the time being, conflicts between surface and groundwater users will most likely continue to be dealt with through laws of more general application—such as environmental review statutes. Some recent legal developments may start to the change this situation, at least somewhat. Recently passed groundwater legislation (SB1168, SB1319 and AB1739) requires a groundwater sustainability agency, where applicable, to include impacts to groundwater-dependent ecosystems in its groundwater sustainability plan. In addition, the law requires such plans to address aquifer draw downs that deplete surface water to such an extent that there is a "significant and unreasonable" effects on beneficial uses of surface water.

In a recent case, a California trial court held that groundwater pumping near the Scott River in northern California has affected river flows and fish, and as such, should be subject to the public trust doctrine. However, the new legislation does not change existing surface or groundwater rights, and it remains to be seen how much of an impact the new case will have. Although the legal wall between surface water and groundwater might be developing a few cracks, that wall still poses an obstacle to the joint management of what is in reality one resource.

The Costs of Overdraft

Some of the costs of groundwater overdraft are borne directly by groundwater pumpers. These costs come from the higher energy costs resulting from pumping deeper groundwater, drilling a deeper or replacement well, and treating declining groundwater quality or finding replacement water supplies. However, much of the time, the costs of groundwater overdraft are borne by other Californians in a variety of ways.

Quantifying the costs of groundwater overdraft is extremely difficult due to limited data collection or sharing in many basins. Most of the information we have on groundwater-related costs are historic or piecemeal in nature.

Some examples of groundwater-related costs include:

Cost of Remediating Land Surface Subsidence

Damages resulting from land subsidence in Santa Clara Valley are estimated at more than $756 million.

In the San Joaquin Valley, damages from subsidence from 1955 to 1972 were estimated to be $1.3 billion (2013 dollars) alone. Total subsidence and costs are expected to be much greater today, but little data are available to quantify total damages.

Cost of Increased Energy Requirements

In 2011, the city of Fresno spent $9 million on electricity to pump groundwater. The increasing costs associated with groundwater pumping have prompted the city to invest in water infrastructure projects to reduce the city's dependence on groundwater.

Agriculture throughout the state has relied on groundwater to supplement the reduction in surface water supplies from the current drought. Total direct and indirect economic losses to statewide agriculture of the drought for this year estimated at $2.2 billion. Within that estimate, additional groundwater pumping costs are estimated to be $454 million.

Other Costs are Harder to Quantify

Diminished surface water flows can occur from extensive groundwater pumping, which means less for surface water users and groundwater-dependent ecosystems such as wetlands, riparian areas, springs and lakes. This impacts an array of ecosystem services. The services provided by the latter, such as water or air quality improvements, have seldom been quantified.

Degraded water quality from aquifer depletion can reduce water supply, requiring alternative supplies, and cause health problems.

Increased food prices are expected from higher energy costs and reduced water reliability.

Recommendations

The impacts of groundwater overdraft are numerous, complex, costly, and have a reach that extends far beyond groundwater pumpers. Broad recognition of the myriad impacts of groundwater overdraft was a key factor in the push for new groundwater legislation in California. Passage of the groundwater bills is a crucial start, but it is only the beginning of the long road ahead to sustainable groundwater management in the state.

> *"There is some grim irony in the huffing and puffing over the impact of the climate change and the danger of carbon emission because we don't pay serious attention to environmental issues until consequences are felt to be too grave to ignore attention."*

Water Scarcity is the Result of Mismanagement

Prasenjit Chowdhury

In the following viewpoint, Prasenjit Chowdhury argues that water scarcity is primarily caused by poor management of water resources. That is the responsibility of government. The author uses India as an example to illustrate this point. Citizens of India are especially vulnerable to water scarcity: Chowdury explains that one of three people at risk of being deprived of water is Indian. The author also asserts that the Indian government should do its best to protect the rights of Indians to clean, safe water. Chowdury is a teacher and commentator on social and political issues affecting India.

"Mismanagement of Water Resources", by Prasenjit Chowdhury, November 5, 2016. Reprinted by permission of Deccan Herald.

As you read, consider the following questions:

1. How many people die daily as a result of lack of safe water?
2. How are Indians especially susceptible to water scarcity?
3. How can the Indian government manage water resources more effectively?

The United Nations designated 2003 as the year of fresh water. There is some grim irony in the huffing and puffing over the impact of the climate change and the danger of carbon emission because we don't pay serious attention to environmental issues until consequences are felt to be too grave to ignore attention. But the warning by the National Centre for Atmospheric Research in Colorado, USA—based on research carried out on the water flow of 925 major rivers from 1948 to 2004—that availability of fresh water could be severely compromised by climate change, is a serious enough prognostication to warrant the fear that future wars on earth are going to be waged over water.

Major sources of fresh water for much of the world's population from the Yellow River in northern China to the Ganges in India to the Colorado river in the United States are in decline as researchers found an overall decline in the amount of water flowing into the world's oceans. Human activities such as the building of dams and the diversion of water for agriculture have attributed largely to the reduction, though climate change was the biggest reason as rising temperatures were altering rainfall patterns and increasing rates of evaporation.

Much as the need to put a cap on the growing carbon emission is expedient, it is necessary to conserve water. Scientists say that 40 per cent of humanity living in South Asia and China could well be living with little drinking water within 50 years as global warming melts Himalayan glaciers, the region's main water source.

It is estimated that 1.3 billion persons in the world don't have access to safe drinking water and some 2.4 billion are denied sanitation and this kills 6,000 people daily. Increasing privatisation of water services in countries like India is leading to growing disparity of access to safe water. The water industry in India is growing at an estimate rate of 25 per cent now. According to 'The Economist', five big food and beverage companies: Nestle, Unilever, Coca-Cola, Anheuser-Busch and Danone, consume almost 575 billion litres of water annually, enough to meet the daily water needs of every person on the planet.

The per capita water availability in India is projected to decline to about 1,140 cubic metres per year in 2050 from 1,820 cubic metres per year (in 2001), the Intergovernmental Panel on Climate Change has stated in a report last year. India's demand for water is growing. It is expected to overtake China's by 2050 when it reaches a staggering 1.6 billion, putting immense strain on its water resources. A rapidly growing economy and a large agricultural sector stretch India's supply of water even thinner.

State's Role

Meanwhile, India's supply of water is rapidly dwindling primarily due to mismanagement of water resources, although over-pumping and pollution are also significant contributors. The state has got a duty to protect ground water against excessive exploitation. It is often felt that the availability of cheap water to the agricultural sector has tended to encourage its pre-emption for a low value, high- volume use, and has encouraged its wasteful and profligate consumption.

The Supreme Court holds that the right to clean air and unpolluted water forms part of the right to life under Article 21 of the Constitution. But every third person deprived of clean water in the world is an Indian. About 86 per cent of all the diseases in the country are directly or indirectly related to the poor quality of drinking water, and 70 per cent of India's water is polluted, according to a report by a non-governmental organisation, the Consumer Unity and Trust Society. In 2003, a World Water Development

Report of the United Nations categorised India among countries with poor quality of water—India ranked 120 among 122 countries.

According to a World Bank report issued in 2005, India will face a severe water crisis in 20 years if the government doesn't change its ways. By 2020, the report says, India's demand for water will exceed all sources of supply. The report sharply takes India to task for lacking in proper water management system in place, while its groundwater is disappearing and river bodies are turning into makeshift sewers. India receives an average of 4,000 billion cubic meters of rainfall every year. Unfortunately, only 48 per cent of rainfall ends up in India's rivers. Due to lack of storage, only 18 per cent can be utilised. So can we really discount our part in the crisis? Could water conservation have a chance with the new government?

> *"With the current water management practices, by 2050 the global agricultural sector will need to double the amount of water used to feed the world. "*

A Combination of Solutions Must Be Used to Solve the Problem of Water Scarcity

Nadia Halim

In the following viewpoint Nadia Halim argues that farmers are being hurt by lack of water availability. There is not one, perfect solution; rather, a combination of approaches must be used. They include using new varieties of crops that require less water, as well as management of crops and soil in a more effective way. Technology also has an important role to play in helping farmers and agricultural workers utilize water more efficiently, the author adds. Halim is a science writer with a background in organic chemistry.

"Agriculture—Meeting the Water Challenge," by Nadia Halim, Water Magazine, John Hopkins Water Institute, January 20, 2017. Reprinted by permission.

As you read, consider the following questions:

1. How much of the Earth's water can be consumed by humans?
2. What are some ways in which the agricultural sector can use water more efficiently?
3. What are the various approaches that can—together— make a difference in water conservation?

Of the vast amount of water that covers the blue earth, 2.5 percent is fresh water, with much of it trapped in glaciers. Only about a third of this resource is economically available for human use. That is a mere teaspoon in a full bathtub when compared to the total amount of water on earth.

Now think about the competing demands on this finite resource—drinking, hygiene, agriculture, energy, and industry in a world of 9.7 billion people by 2050[1]. Add to that the predicted effects of climate change. Despite global increases in rainfall, many dry regions including the Mediterranean, Middle East, and Africa will suffer badly from reduced rainfall and increased evaporation[2]. It quickly becomes clear that without better water management strategies today, the world is headed for a crisis that will affect every aspect of life.

Currently, at least 1.8 billion people use a water source contaminated with feces. As a result, an estimated 842, 000 people die each year from diarrhea caused by unsafe drinking water, improper sanitation, and lack of hand washing[3]. Though the effects of water shortage are more severe in the developing world, the United States and Europe haven't escaped unscathed. In California, officials reported that the state entered its fourth year of drought in 2015, which was the driest since meteorological records began. At the same time, per capita water use has continued to rise.

The public usually associates water shortages with a lack of drinking water. But global water scarcity has a critical impact on food security. Water is the biggest limiting factor in the world's ability to feed a growing population and the link between food, energy, climate, economic growth, and human security challenges.

Roughly, a liter of water is required to produce every calorie, so an adequate daily diet requires more than 2,000 liters of water to produce enough food for one person. Currently, agriculture utilizes on average 70 percent of the world's available fresh water. But this is higher in areas such as the Middle East and northern Africa, where up to 90 percent of freshwater withdrawals are used to irrigate crops.[4]

In many parts of the world, mismanagement is depleting freshwater resources—the blue water in rivers, lakes, and groundwater stores—which in turn has threatened freshwater biodiversity and permanently changed patterns of water flow. If we continue to apply current water management practices, by 2050 the global agricultural sector will need to double the amount of water used to feed the world.[5]

With a finite amount of freshwater and increasing demand, both in quantity and variety of uses, the need for water resources protection and management has never been greater. The question is how do we meet this challenge without increasing fresh water withdrawal to feed the world?

Increasing Water Efficiency on the Farm

Our best option is to implement solutions that have the potential of increasing the efficiency, equity, and sustainability of water use. This will require a shift from the focus on pure "land productivity" without concern for water use, to "water productivity," that is, getting the highest yield out of every drop of water used in agriculture. Resource efficient methods and technology will allow farmers to grow more food with less water, while protecting biodiversity.

Irrigation holds the most promise for increasing food productivity and security, provided it is managed efficiently. However, about 40 percent of water used in irrigation is wasted through unsustainable practices such as field flooding. Flooded rice paddies, for example, traditionally use on average about 2,500 liters of water to produce 1 kg of rough rice. As agricultural water scarcity increases, there is a growing need for water saving technologies such as aerobic rice (varieties that grow well in unflooded fields).

Modern irrigation systems can drastically reduce the amount of water squandered by efficiently delivering water directly to plants. This reduces the amount of water lost through surface evaporation by 30 to 70 percent depending on the crop and weather conditions.

The second part of the equation comes from the rainfall that infiltrates and remains in the soil, called green water. This is the largest fresh water resource and the basis of rain-fed agriculture. While farmers cannot control how much it rains, they can do a lot to retain rain in the soil. All rain-fed agriculture depends on the soil's capacity to capture rain water. Heavy rain cannot penetrate parched, crusted soil and just runs off the surface.

Modest measures like conservation tillage practices that improve soil structure by avoiding plowing, mulching to prevent evaporation, and small-scale water harvesting can increase rain-water infiltration by as much as 2-3 fold. Thus, farmers must integrate a combination of rain-fed and irrigated agricultural methods to optimize the yields of crops for the water used.

Complementing water conservation techniques are new crop varieties, which use water more efficiently and tolerate heat and drought better. In the past, breeders have slowly improved crop varieties by crossing pairs of plants that exhibit desirable qualities. Now this slow and labor-intensive method is getting a helping hand from molecular biology. Researchers are saving time by examining plant DNA for clues to predict which plant crosses are most likely to be successful in producing a given trait. Genetic modification is another tool used to improve seeds in such a way that they can produce the same or more yield with less water.

Today's crop protection technologies can also help plants use water more efficiently. Some products have a beneficial effect on root systems, allowing plants to make the most of available water and cope better in dry periods. Plant regulator products are designed to help prevent crop loss when plants grow too tall and collapse. They also provide additional benefits by reducing water needed to grow crops. Other products are specifically designed to protect plants from moderate drought and other stresses by blocking the plant's response to stress, which increases the long-term health of plants and improves farmers' yields.

Integrated Approach to Address the Water Challenge

There is no silver bullet—no one answer to addressing the global water challenge. But an integrated approach using the technologies outlined here and tailored to the local conditions, crops, and farmers can maximize water use efficiency. With this, comes the responsibility to prevent run off of agricultural chemicals into streams, rivers, and ground water aquifers.

Farmers will not only produce more food, but also become stewards of the land, protecting against rain run-off, soil erosion, water stress on plants, flooding, and desertification of arable land. Desertification is the process by which fertile land is degraded to the point it can no longer grow crops, typically as a result of drought, deforestation, or intensive agricultural practices.

Water efficiency measures using existing agricultural technology can sustainably increase net water availability, at a reasonable cost. In comparison, trying to increase water supply often requires energy-intensive measures such as desalination, which are vastly more expensive than the efficiency measures outlined here.[6]

To better manage the competing demands for water, agricultural policies will have to make water efficiency a priority. This will require investment in research to develop innovative water-efficient technologies in addition to drought tolerant seeds, new crop protection products, and optimized irrigation systems for specific crops. But the best and most innovative technology is useless if farmers cannot afford it, see no advantage to it, or do not understand it.

Therefore, a key component of policymaking will have to include infrastructure for knowledge sharing and access to technology. The Food and Agriculture Organization of the United Nations estimates that over the next 40 years irrigation will require a cumulative investment of almost $1 trillion. Governments, NGOs, and public-private partnerships should facilitate implementing technology on the farm where better water management is critical for food production and the environment. This includes access to affordable credit and financial risk-management mechanisms, such as insurance for weather-related crop losses.

Already the benefits of this model can be seen in partnerships between developed country governments, international organizations, and private companies, which are helping small farms with access to finance, guaranteed markets, technical assistance, and insurance.

Enabling individuals and communities to understand their options for managing water, to choose from these options, and to take responsibility for their choices could positively alter the way the world uses its limited water resources.

References

1 The World Population Prospects: 2015 Revision, United Nations Department of Economic and Social Affairs

2 Climate Change and Water, Intergovernmental Panel on Climate Change, 2008.

3 WHO/UNICEF Joint Monitoring Programme for Water Supply and Sanitation, 2015

4 FAO Aquastat, 2005, World Resource and Earthscan "Water for food, water for life" Institute

5 The Economist, "The 9-billion People Question," February 26, 2011.

6 2030 Water Resources Group; Charting our Water Future, Economic framework to inform decision-making; Dec 2009; http://www.2030waterresourcesgroup.com/water_full

Periodical and Internet Sources Bibliography

The following articles have been selected to supplement the diverse views presented in this chapter.

The Climate Reality Project, "The Facts about Climate Change and Drought," June 15, 2016. http://www.climaterealityproject.org/blog/facts-about-climate-change-and-drought

Conserve Energy Future, "Causes of Water Scarcity." http://www.conserve-energy-future.com/causes-effects-solutions-of-water-scarcity.php

Alexandra E. V. Evans, Dr. Munir A. Hanjra, Yunlu Jiang, Dr. Manzoor Qadir & Pay Drechsel, "Water pollution in Asia: The Urgent Need for Prevention and Monitoring," Global Water Forum, June 9, 2012. http://www.globalwaterforum.org/2012/06/09/water-pollution-in-asia-the-urgent-need-for-prevention-and-monitoring/

International Food Policy Research Institute, "What's Really Causing Water Scarcity in Africa South of the Sahara?" August 29, 2013. http://www.ifpri.org/blog/what%E2%80%99s-really-causing-water-scarcity-africa-south-sahara

Sonia Luthra and Amrita Kundu, "India's Water Crisis: Causes and Cures," The National Bureau of Asian Research, August 13, 2013. http://www.nbr.org/research/activity.aspx?id=356

National Drought Mitigation Center, "Causes of Drought." http://drought.unl.edu/DroughtforKids/WhatisDrought/CausesofDrought.aspx

PBS, "What's Causing Water Shortages in Ghana, Nigeria?" March 15, 2012. http://www.pbs.org/newshour/bb/globalhealth-jan-june12-westafrica_03-15/

Mandakini Devasher Surie, "South Asia's Water Crisis: A Problem of Scarcity Amid Abundance," March 25, 2015. http://asiafoundation.org/2015/03/25/south-asias-water-crisis-a-problem-of-scarcity-amid-abundance/

US Geological Survey, "Droughts: Questions and Answers." https://water.usgs.gov/edu/qadroughts.html

Gayathri Vaidyanathan, "Fracking Can Contaminate Water," Scientific American, April 4, 2016. https://www.scientificamerican.com/article/fracking-can-contaminate-drinking-water/

CHAPTER 3

How Is Water Used as a Political Tool?

Chapter Preface

G overnments are formed for the protection of their citizens: for the protection and security of their property, their jobs, and their very lives. More and more, as fresh and safe water becomes a resource that people can no longer take for granted, governments are beginning to make water into a political issue.

In India and Pakistan, for example, water scarcity is causing political chaos. Both nations derive much of their freshwater from the rivers that flow to the Indus basin. If a river runs through a nation's borders, can that nation build a dam to collect the water, even if the neighboring nation also depends on the water? In other words, nations have always clearly demarcated their land boundaries, but in the future they may also need to find ways to delineate their water sources.

The political turmoil over water resources is exploding in many other parts of the world: in Israel and the occupied Palestinian territories, Palestinians accuse Israel of diverting water from the Jordan River to Israeli settlements and away from Palestinian villages. The water diversion and drought have caused the Jordan River to dry up. The Jordan River, unfortunately, also supplies fresh water to the neighboring nation of Jordan (which is largely desert). Meanwhile, in China, water scarcity has prompted the government to build large dams to collect water; some of those dams are preventing water from flowing to Tibet—effectively, depriving Tibet of its primary source of fresh water. In Ireland, the government tried to impose a tax on water, and the action led to angry demonstrations.

Economic rules apply to water: when something is scarce, but in high demand, its price increases. As water becomes less and less available, it will become more valuable, and whoever controls it has the potential to make a tremendous profit. It could lead to situations where companies or individuals claim or own water rights over other segments of a population who don't agree with them politically.

Furthermore, on a global scale, the value of water can also bring nations to the brink of war, if they need to fight for their survival. For regions of the world that are already feeling the stress of water scarcity, the availability of safe water is causing tensions to rise. Government leaders are starting to view water as an essential tool and strategy in their diplomatic relationships with other nations. For example, claiming water advantages, such as damming up a river before its waters reach a neighboring nation, can be used to pressure or to defeat political opponents.

This chapter will examine the various ways in which water is currently being debated as a political issue. It offers case studies of how water is being politicized in various regions of the world, such as sub-saharan Africa and India, as well as right here in the United States of America.

> *"Already a billion people, or one in seven people on the planet, lack access to safe drinking water."*

Global Water Shortages Pose Threat of Terror and War

Suzanne Goldenberg

In the following viewpoint, Suzanne Goldenberg describes the results of a 2014 scientific study in which scientists learned how depleted groundwater reserves have become. Goldenberg cites a US national intelligence report warning that the mismanagement of water resources in other nations could cause global conflicts as well as security problems for the United States. Using these data, Goldenberg argues that water scarcity leads to competition and a shortage of food production and industry, which can threaten a nation's survival. Goldenberg is the U.S. environment correspondent for the Guardian and has won awards for her reports from the Middle East.

As you read, consider the following questions:

1. How has mismanagement of water lead to the current water crisis, according to Goldenberg?
2. Why are the groundwater reserves being depleted?
3. How can violent confrontations, on a national and a local level, be sparked by water scarcity?

On 17 January, scientists downloaded fresh data from a pair of NASA satellites and distributed the findings among the small group of researchers who track the world's water reserves. At the University of California, Irvine, hydrologist James Famiglietti looked over the data from the gravity-sensing Grace satellites with a rising sense of dread.

The data, released last week, showed California on the verge of an epic drought, with its backup systems of groundwater reserves so run down that the losses could be picked up by satellites orbiting 400km above the Earth's surface.

"It was definitely an 'oh my gosh moment," Famiglietti said. "The groundwater is our strategic reserve. It's our backup, and so where do you go when the backup is gone?"

That same day, the state governor, Jerry Brown, declared a drought emergency and appealed to Californians to cut their water use by 20%. "Every day this drought goes on we are going to have to tighten the screws on what people are doing," he said.

Seventeen rural communities are in danger of running out of water within 60 days and that number is expected to rise, after the main municipal water distribution system announced it did not have enough supplies and would have to turn off the taps to local agencies.

There are other shock moments ahead—and not just for California—in a world where water is increasingly in short supply because of growing demands from agriculture, an expanding population, energy production and climate change.

Already a billion people, or one in seven people on the planet, lack access to safe drinking water. Britain, of course, is currently at the other extreme. Great swaths of the country are drowning in misery, after a series of Atlantic storms off the south-western coast. But that too is part of the picture that has been coming into sharper focus over 12 years of the Grace satellite record. Countries at northern latitudes and in the tropics are getting wetter. But those countries at mid-latitude are running increasingly low on water.

"What we see is very much a picture of the wet areas of the Earth getting wetter," Famiglietti said. "Those would be the high latitudes like the Arctic and the lower latitudes like the tropics. The middle latitudes in between, those are already the arid and semi-arid parts of the world and they are getting drier."

On the satellite images the biggest losses were denoted by red hotspots, he said. And those red spots largely matched the locations of groundwater reserves.

"Almost all of those red hotspots correspond to major aquifers of the world. What Grace shows us is that groundwater depletion is happening at a very rapid rate in almost all of the major aquifers in the arid and semi-arid parts of the world."

The Middle East, north Africa and south Asia are all projected to experience water shortages over the coming years because of decades of bad management and overuse.

Watering crops, slaking thirst in expanding cities, cooling power plants, fracking oil and gas wells—all take water from the same diminishing supply. Add to that climate change—which is projected to intensify dry spells in the coming years—and the world is going to be forced to think a lot more about water than it ever did before.

The losses of water reserves are staggering. In seven years, beginning in 2003, parts of Turkey, Syria, Iraq and Iran along the Tigris and Euphrates rivers lost 144 cubic kilometres of stored freshwater—or about the same amount of water in the Dead Sea, according to data compiled by the Grace mission and released last year.

A small portion of the water loss was due to soil drying up because of a 2007 drought and to a poor snowpack. Another share was lost to evaporation from lakes and reservoirs. But the majority of the water lost, $90km^3$, or about 60%, was due to reductions in groundwater.

Farmers, facing drought, resorted to pumping out groundwater—at times on a massive scale. The Iraqi government drilled about 1,000 wells to weather the 2007 drought, all drawing from the same stressed supply.

In south Asia, the losses of groundwater over the last decade were even higher. About 600 million people live on the 2,000km swath that extends from eastern Pakistan, across the hot dry plains of northern India and into Bangladesh, and the land is the most intensely irrigated in the world. Up to 75% of farmers rely on pumped groundwater to water their crops, and water use is intensifying.

Over the last decade, groundwater was pumped out 70% faster than in the 1990s. Satellite measurements showed a staggering loss of 54km³ of groundwater a year. Indian farmers were pumping their way into a water crisis.

The US security establishment is already warning of potential conflicts—including terror attacks—over water. In a 2012 report the US director of national intelligence warned that overuse of water—as in India and other countries—was a source of conflict that could potentially compromise US national security.

The report focused on water basins critical to the US security regime—the Nile, Tigris-Euphrates, Mekong, Jordan, Indus, Brahmaputra and Amu Darya. It concluded: "During the next 10 years, many countries important to the United States will experience water problems—shortages, poor water quality, or floods—that will risk instability and state failure, increase regional tensions, and distract them from working with the United States."

Water, on its own, was unlikely to bring down governments. But the report warned that shortages could threaten food production and energy supply and put additional stress on governments struggling with poverty and social tensions.

Some of those tensions are already apparent on the ground. The Pacific Institute, which studies issues of water and global security, found a fourfold increase in violent confrontations over water over the last decade. "I think the risk of conflicts over water is growing—not shrinking—because of increased competition, because of bad management and, ultimately, because of the impacts of climate change," said Peter Gleick, president of the Pacific Institute.

There are dozens of potential flashpoints, spanning the globe. In the Middle East, Iranian officials are making contingency plans for water rationing in the greater Tehran area, home to 22 million people.

Egypt has demanded Ethiopia stop construction of a mega-dam on the Nile, vowing to protect its historical rights to the river at "any cost". The Egyptian authorities have called for a study into whether the project would reduce the river's flow.

Jordan, which has the third lowest reserves in the region, is struggling with an influx of Syrian refugees. The country is undergoing power cuts because of water shortages. Last week, Prince Hassan, the uncle of King Abdullah, warned that a war over water and energy could be even bloodier than the Arab spring.

The United Arab Emirates, faced with a growing population, has invested in desalination projects and is harvesting rainwater. At an international water conference in Abu Dhabi last year, Crown Prince General Sheikh Mohammed bin Zayed al-Nahyan said: "For us, water is [now] more important than oil."

The chances of countries going to war over water were slim—at least over the next decade, the national intelligence report said. But it warned ominously: "As water shortages become more acute beyond the next 10 years, water in shared basins will increasingly be used as leverage; the use of water as a weapon or to further terrorist objectives will become more likely beyond 10 years."

Gleick predicted such conflicts would take other trajectories. He expected water tensions would erupt on a more local scale.

"I think the biggest worry today is sub-national conflicts—conflicts between farmers and cities, between ethnic groups, between pastoralists and farmers in Africa, between upstream users and downstream users on the same river," said Gleick.

"We have more tools at the international level to resolve disputes between nations. We have diplomats. We have treaties.

We have international organisations that reduce the risk that India and Pakistan will go to war over water but we have far fewer tools at the sub-national level."

And new fault lines are emerging with energy production. America's oil and gas rush is putting growing demands on a water supply already under pressure from drought and growing populations.

More than half the nearly 40,000 wells drilled since 2011 were in drought-stricken areas, a report from the Ceres green investment network found last week. About 36% of those wells were in areas already experiencing groundwater depletion.

How governments manage those water problems—and protect their groundwater reserves—will be critical. When California emerged from its last prolonged dry spell, in 2010, the Sacramento and San Joaquin river basins were badly depleted. The two river basins lost 10km3 of freshwater each year in 2012 and 2013, dropping the total volume of snow, surface water, soil moisture and groundwater to the lowest levels in nearly a decade.

Without rain, those reservoirs are projected to drop even further during this drought. State officials are already preparing to drill additional wells to draw on groundwater. Famiglietti said that would be a mistake.

"We are standing on a cliff looking over the edge and we have to decide what we are going to do," he said.

"Are we just going to plunge into this next epic drought and tremendous, never-before-seen rates of groundwater depletion, or are we going to buckle down and start thinking of managing critical reserve for the long term? We are standing on a precipice here."

"*The wars may be over the use of water, over its sharing, over who gets how much. This war plays out each day, all the time, in countless Indian cities, towns, and villages.*"

Water Scarcity Leads to Internal Strife for Nations

Pallava Bagla

In the following viewpoint, Pallava Bagla offers some insight into the water crisis in India, providing compelling statistics about the growing tensions over the availability of safe water. Bagla points out that India's population is part of the problem: the nation has 17 percent of the world's population, with over 1 billion people, but only 4 percent of the world's fresh water sources. Complicating matters are a growing pollution issue as well as a monsoon season that will provide less rainfall than in previous years. The only solution is good governance and management of the precious little water that is available, according to Bagla, to prevent local politics and fighting. Bagla is Science Editor for New Delhi Television and a globally recognized science writer.

"Placing Clean Water at the Heart of Good Governance in India," by Pallava Bagla, Ministry of External Affairs, Government of India, August 15, 2014. Reprinted by permission.

As you read, consider the following questions:

1. What is the spiritual importance of water in India?
2. What factors are contributing to water scarcity in India?
3. How can water be managed effectively in India, despite the large population?

In water, there is life and without water, there is no life. Water is almost a producer of life. From thick jungles where diverse plants and animals throng to human settlements that naturally seek water and cluster around it forever; this is one natural resource that is at the core of life on Earth. Today more than ever the new Prime Minister Narendra Modi led government is placing clean water at the heart of good governance. So when Prime Minister Narendra Modi gave a clarion call on July 29, 2014 when speaking to agriculture specialists seeking 'per drop, more crop', it automatically touches a chord among Indians.

Personally I have often wondered whether it is blood that runs through my veins, or is it that elixir of life my parched ancestors describe as liquid gold? Even as a child, when I learnt from my father of our roots, which traced back to Churu, a small township in the desert state of Rajasthan in western India, where summer temperatures soar up to 50 degrees Centigrade, it was the dryness and utter lack of water that caught in my throat. Discomfiting, questioning, always—till I began to feel and sense the enormous abuse of water in average daily human life—for I spent many wildly happy hours of my childhood on the banks of the holiest of the Indian rivers the Ganga.

Fresh potable water is at a premium and may possibly become the rate-determining step in the future. India with over a 1.2 billion people makes up almost 17 percent of the world's population—the contrast is that the country possesses merely 4 percent of the world's fresh water resources with the renewable fresh water resources of India standing at 1869 billion cubic meters (BCM) per year. Currently every Indian has access to less than a fourth of what is the world average and disparities are only growing. Can this thirsty divide between the water-starved and the water-rich be bridged with sound water management and by deploying best practices.

There is a huge renewed interest in cleaning the river Ganga with the new National Democratic Alliance government even renaming the central water ministry as the `Ministry for Water Resources, River Development and Ganga Rejuvenation'. On July 7, 2014 a large inter-ministerial national consultation called `Ganga Manthan' was organized in New Delhi where it was recommended that a honest effort will be made that in next five years a clean free flowing Ganga is given back to Indians. The new government is undoubtedly focusing heavily on providing clean water, towards that a massive effort to clean up India's National river the Ganga has been allocated $ 340 million in the budget, the 2500 kilometer long northern Indian river whose basin houses some 400 million people, has been heavily polluted and Modi promises to clean it up by 2019. He made this promise while giving a victory speech on the banks of the Ganga from his own constituency in Varanasi.

According to estimates by the Ministry of Water `the per capita availability of water in the country is 1545 cubic meters as per the 2011 census. The per capita water availability in the country is reducing progressively due to increase in population. The average annual per capita availability of water in the country, taking into consideration the population of the country as per the 2001 census, was 1816 cubic meters which reduced to 1545 cubic meters as per the 2011 census.'

According to estimates put out by the National Water Development Agency (NWDA) to meet the irrigation potential of 160 million hectares by 2050 up from the current of about 100 million hectares, new strategies will have to be adopted especially since India's population is likely to be anywhere between 1.4 to 1.5 billion up from the current 1.2 billion. To feed the people by then the country will have to produce some 450 million tons of food grains, almost doubling the output in less than four decades.

Ensuing that the country gets more crop per drop will the big game changer.

A government report states that `due to limited availability of water, but growing demand of water due to increasing population, urbanization and industrialization. India is facing water stress. In addition due to contamination of water sources and poor water treatment facility it is often difficult to get safe drinking water.' All of these are to be tackled at a war footing.

Today, a truant monsoon is causing some heartburn in India. The monsoon rainfall is the harbinger of life in the Sub-continent affecting the lives of nearly a quarter of the world's population, so it is not surprising that India has been trying to forecast the summer monsoon for over a century, not always succeeding in predicting droughts.

To make the long-range forecasts of the monsoon more accurate, India has launched a $ 75 million, 5-year research program called the `monsoon mission' to decipher the mystery of the monsoon. The southwest monsoon is that life-giving phenomenon which showers on the Indian landmass 80% of the total annual of 105 cm rainfall that India receives. Every year between June-September, moisture-laden winds blowing in from the Indian Ocean rejuvenate the parched Indian countryside. The monsoon arrives without fail, but forecasting it months ahead is a nightmare. The drought of 2002 shrank India's GDP by an estimated 5.8%. Calling the monsoon an `intriguing phenomenon'. Shailesh Nayak, a geologist and secretary for the Ministry of Earth Sciences says `understanding the monsoon is a major priority for the next five years'.

According to the government `water quality data of various river stretches has revealed that organic pollution particularly Bio-chemical Oxygen Demand (BOD) has exceeded the desired water quality criteria in 150 river stretches covering 121 rivers. The major cause of rising organic pollution, particularly BOD in these rivers, is due to discharge of untreated and partially treated domestic effluents by various municipalities across the country.

Pollution abatement in rivers is an ongoing and collective effort of the central and state governments. Ministry of Environment & Forests, Government of India is supplementing the efforts of the state governments in pollution abatement in various rivers through the centrally sponsored National River Conservation Plan (NRCP), which presently covers 40 rivers in 190 towns spread over 20 States. Pollution abatement schemes include interception, diversion and treatment of sewage; low cost sanitation works on riverbanks; gas fired, electric or at times improved wood crematoria are being used. Sewage treatment capacity of 4574 million liters per day has been created. Nobody can doubt that rivers in India are heavily polluted and giving them a quick scrub will certainly make India a healthier place.

And yet, through all the haze, is undying worship the likes of which was witnessed at the world's largest ever gathering of human beings on Earth at the 2013 Kumbh mela in Allahabad that numbered well over 30 million. When one witnesses the power of that simple down to Earth worship, one can easily pack up all concerns and stand up to celebrate—for that is what water is all about.

Yet, the devout still throw remnants of their religious ceremonies into the river closest to them, perhaps in the hope that the river, and its swirling (or sometimes disturbingly stagnant) water, in its inherent magnanimity, will pardon all, will absorb the overload, and will continue to throb and flow and provide. The even more devout throng to the Maha Kumbh every few years in lifelong praise of water, whether they are the primordial Naga sadhus or ordinary unsung housewives who spend whole lives collecting and preserving Ganga water in their homes. I ask myself that question very often—what does water really mean to me? Everything, perhaps. I remember how, in 2002, when India was reeling under a terrible drought, the economy took a real beating. And as I traveled, I saw the power of water, and of communities that rose to create and conserve water, in the villages of Alwar in

Rajasthan rejuvenating a long lost river with the active participation of the local communities.

The whole spirit of water is of tranquility and peace, praise and cleansing. Yet, there are wars, and it is predicted they have only just begun. The wars may be over the use of water, over its sharing, over who gets how much. This war plays out each day, all the time, in countless Indian cities, towns, and villages. Its many scenes are depicted in the long and tired queues of women with more pitchers than they can hold, in the growing frequency of water tankers that actually sell water in many parts of the country, and in the larger political dramas that unfold around the sharing of rivers between states and the damming of water.

But water endures, and also manages to push human endurance beyond limits. It befriends, pacifies, cajoles and makes its way into the lives of the unlikeliest of people. It draws humans, animals and plants alike. It can make or break ecosystems and economies. It entices industry and beckons even the atheist. Water is at what must truly be the center of the Universe for every Indian. Better governance of this vital resource will ensure a healthy and prosperous future for India.

> "Human rights laws guaranteeing
> the right to water are not strong
> enough to adequately deter countries
> that may consider engaging in
> water wars."

Water Scarcity in Central Asia May Lead to Conflict

Emily Singer Hurvitz

In the following viewpoint, Emily Singer Hurvitz describes the way in which water scarcity is becoming a major point of tension in Central Asia, specifically over control of the Amu Darya and the Syr Darya rivers. Tajikistan and Kyrgyzstan control the rivers, and they are planning to dam them to create reservoirs. The neighboring nations of Uzbekistan and Kazakhstan are worried that these actions will cause their own water resources to dry up. Hurvitz is a human rights lawyer.

"Water Scarcity in Central Asia May Lead to Conflict," by Emily Singer Hurvitz, The Human Rights Brief, November 14, 2012. Reprinted by permission.

As you read, consider the following questions:

1. What is the historical arrangement agreed to by Central Asian nations for water sharing?
2. Are the international agreements regulating water access legally binding?
3. Why is it important to recognize water access as a human right?

Water scarcity is a looming problem throughout the world, particularly affecting developing nations such as the Central Asian states. Approximately 884 million people do not have access to safe drinking water and the number of people affected by severe water stress could increase to over 3.9 billion by 2030. In Central Asia, obtaining an equitable division of the region's major rivers, the Amu Darya and the Syr Darya, is a disputed issue that may lead to armed conflict. Tajikistan and Kyrgyzstan, the countries that control the rivers, both have plans to build hydroelectric dams, which will give them substantial influence over water resources in the region, to the potential detriment of Uzbekistan and Kazakhstan. With increasing water scarcity in Central Asia and the vacuum left by a lack of binding international law, the dam plans will make achieving the seventh UN Millennium Development Goal, ensuring widespread access to clean water, and realizing the objective of UN Resolution 64/292 on the right to water, increasingly difficult and may send the region into armed conflict. The effects of such a conflict could be devastating, leading to the contravention of the Convention on the Rights of the Child (CRC) and the Convention on the Elimination of All Forms of Discrimination Against Women (CEDAW).

Historically, the Central Asian states developed a standard for water and electricity exchange due to stringent Soviet resource-allocation policies. This arrangement controlled the potential effects that uneven water distribution would have on human security in the region. In 1992, after the fall of the Soviet Union, the newly independent Central Asian states signed the Almaty Agreement, maintaining the Soviet allocation of water, which favored Kazakhstan and Uzbekistan. Under the agreement, Tajikistan and Kyrgyzstan do not have enough water for their planned development activities and are desperately in need of the dam projects.

Because the right to water is not a self-standing right in international human rights law, dam projects by Tajikistan and Kyrgyzstan would not necessarily be in direct contravention to binding international obligations. The proposed dam projects will provide Tajikistan and Kyrgyzstan with a steady stream of urgently needed power. Despite this, Uzbek leadership, with Kazakh support, opposes the dam projects, arguing that they will disrupt water supplies in the two countries, negatively affecting their economies by reducing the amount of water they have for agriculture to export, and damaging the environment. If Tajikistan and Kyrgyzstan move forward with their dam projects, achieving the seventh MDG to "halve the proportion of the population without sustainable access to safe drinking water and basic sanitation by 2015" will be nearly impossible. It will also challenge the goals set out in UN General Assembly Resolution 64/292, which promises "to provide safe, clean, accessible and affordable drinking water and sanitation for all." Though Tajikistan and Kyrgyzstan both agreed to the MDGs and voted for the General Assembly resolution, neither of these declarations is legally binding.

Despite the lack of binding international guarantees for the right to water, Tajikistan and Kyrgyzstan may reconsider moving forward with their dam projects because of the threat of war. Uzbekistan's president, Islam Karimov, stated that the dam projects could lead to war because of water's importance to Uzbekistan's agricultural exports, which make up a large percentage of the country's foreign earnings. Water conflicts, or "water wars," occur when a country controls the water resources of another, water-scarce, country and uses water as leverage over the country that does not control its own access to water. Human rights laws guaranteeing the right to water are not strong enough to adequately deter countries that may consider engaging in water wars. However, the humanitarian effects of water wars may trigger international legal obligations. Women and children in Central Asia are particularly in danger from water scarcity issues because much of the agricultural work falls on them. They are often responsible for transporting water to the home; thus, with increased water scarcity they will be spending much more time and energy transporting water. Additionally there is clear gender inequality regarding access to water, with rural women facing critical problems in this area. Despite the lack of binding international law on the right to water, by instating policies that will exacerbate water scarcity and lead to war, the Central Asian states are ignoring Article 14 of CEDAW and Article 24 of the CRC, which specifically protect the rights of women and children and their access to water resources.

The countries of Central Asia are victims of a post-Soviet lack of a coordinated management system, but these actions could likely hamper the goals set out in human rights declarations. Without stronger human rights laws governing access to water, the region is highly susceptible to water wars, certain countries and minorities are disproportionately affected, and water scarcity will get exponentially worse due to climate change and mismanagement of resources.

> "*Both sets of officials felt that without political will at the top, transboundary water disputes between India and Pakistan could not be resolved by hydrologists and bureaucrats.*"

Water Can Be a Source of Disagreement Among Neighboring Nations

The Third Pole

In the following viewpoint, the growing tension between India and Pakistan is detailed and explained. The two nations signed the Indus Water Treaty in 1960 to help govern the availability and use of water provided by the rivers that flow into the Indus Basin. However, India wants to build hydropower plants that require the use of water, which Pakistan is currently disputing. Pakistan also alleges that India is delaying the final resolution of the problem as a way to stall the process as it builds the power plants. The viewpoint highlights the many diplomatic and political problems that can be triggered when water is at stake. The Third Pole is a multilingual platform dedicated to promoting information and discussion about the Himalayan watershed and the rivers that originate there.

"Indus Water Dispute Going to Arbitrators Again," The Third Pole, July 18, 2016. https://www.thethirdpole.net/2016/07/18/indus-water-dispute-going-to-arbitrators-again/.

As you read, consider the following questions:

1. What is the two-part problem being disputed?
2. What role can the International Court of Arbitration play in resolving this conflict?
3. What is implied by the fact that there must be "political will at the top" to ease the tensions over water usage?

India and Pakistan have once again failed to resolve their differences over two hydropower projects being built in India. The Indian government holds that the Kishanganga and Ratle projects are being built within the ambit of the 1960 Indus Waters Treaty (IWT) between the two countries. Pakistan does not agree, and has decided to take the matter to the Hague-based International Court of Arbitration (ICA).

Under the treaty, Pakistan holds the right to the water of the three western rivers in the Indus basin (the Indus, Jhelum and Chenab) and the rights to the eastern rivers belong to India. About 80% of the water that flowed through these six rivers in the 1950s was allocated to Pakistan. However, India has certain non-consumptive use rights over the waters of the western rivers

The latest deadlock came after two days of talks on July 14-15 between the IWT commissioners and officials of the two countries in New Delhi. After the talks, Pakistan's Water and Power Minister Khawaja Mohammad Asif tweeted that his government would go to the ICA.

A spokesperson of India's Ministry of External Affairs described Pakistan's plan as a violation of the IWT, which asks the two countries to resolve their differences through bilateral discussions as far as possible. New Delhi believes more discussions would lead to a solution, and it would be unnecessary to drag the matter to the ICA.

Pakistan's minister said talks with India on both projects had continued for two and half years at the Permanent Commission of Indus Waters (PCIW), but this could not yield results.

THE POLITICS OF WATER

The World Economic Forum has ranked water crises as the most worrying global threat, more dangerous than terrorist attacks or financial meltdowns, and more likely to occur than the use of weapons of mass destruction. And research by the Strategic Foresight Group has shown the importance of wise management: Countries engaged in the joint stewardship of water resources are exceedingly unlikely to go to war.

Countries sharing rivers in Africa, South-East Asia and Latin America have recognized that national interests and regional stability can be mutually reinforcing if human needs are given priority over chauvinism.

Last fall, the international community adopted the UN's Sustainable Development Goals (SDGs), which promise to "ensure availability and sustainable management of water and sanitation for all". Part of this pledge is a commitment to "expand international cooperation".

Those in charge of implementing this commitment must bear in mind that water cooperation is not merely about signing treaties and holding meetings. It also entails jointly planning infrastructure projects, managing floods and droughts, developing an integrated strategy to combat climate change, ensuring the quality of water courses and holding regular summits to negotiate trade-offs between water and other public goods.

For poor people in the developing world, such transboundary cooperation generates significant dividends. When countries agree on the construction and management of critical infrastructure, there are no delays. Costs are saved. Benefits are shared in an optimum way. If all developing countries with shared river basins embraced transboundary cooperation, their GDP growth easily could rise by a percentage point.

Finally, international law should be designed to prevent, not just resolve, conflicts. In particular, a robust global treaty is needed to regulate emissions into bodies of water. Today, most disagreements over water concern quantity. In the future, conflicts will increasingly be about water quality, as irrigation practices, industrialization and urbanization contribute to rising pollution levels.

"The Politics of Water," by Sundeep Waslekar, HT Media Limited, March 21, 2016.

The IWT says that when water disputes fail to get resolved bilaterally, the government that feels aggrieved has the option to go to the ICA; if there is a dispute over the design of any project, the government should go to a neutral expert.

Pakistani newspapers quoted officials as saying the country's water rights were being violated by India on two rivers, the Chenab and the Jhelum, through a "faulty design" of the 850 MW Ratle and 330 MW Kishanganga hydropower projects, both located before the rivers reach Pakistan.

The Dispute

The current dispute is over two issues: first, whether India can draw down the water in the reservoirs below the dead storage level in any event other than an unforeseen emergency; second, whether India's diversion of water for the run-of-the-river projects was a violation of the IWT. There are four other technical questions on the design of the Indian projects which are still unresolved.

India has consistently maintained that the design will continue to supply Pakistan the 43 million acre feet every day, as it is supposed to do under the treaty, and as it has done right through, even when the two countries were at war.

But the eight-member Pakistani delegation led by Water and Power Secretary Mohammad Younas Dagha was not satisfied with the talks.

There were critics of Pakistan's decision within the country. Jamiat Ali Shah, former Pakistan commissioner for the IWT, expressed "strong reservations" about the government going to the ICA "at this belated stage" and especially about including the Kishanganga project, which is ready to be commissioned this November.

Past Court Ruling Gave Green Light

Located on a tributary to the Jhelum, the USD 864 million Kishanganga project is a run-of-the-river hydropower scheme that is designed to divert water from the Kishanganga river (called

Neelum in Pakistan), generate electricity, and then send the water back to the river.

Construction began in 2007, but was halted in 2011 because Pakistan went to the ICA and said the Kishanganga project would adversely affect the Neelum Jhelum hydropower project it planned on the same river. The Pakistani government said its project had been on the boards since 1989, long before the Kishanganga project was conceived, though it had been able to raise the money to start work.

In February 2013, the ICA gave an interim ruling that India could divert a minimum amount of water for power generation, and work on the Kishanganga project was resumed. The ICA confirmed its ruling in December 2013.

Going by the IWT, the ICA now has to find seven arbitrators – two each from India and Pakistan and three jointly or by institutions listed in the treaty. Jamiat Ali Shah feels the Kishanganga project will be launched before the seven arbitrators are in place.

Shah told the Pakistani media that in the past, India had used delaying tactics in response to Pakistani objections and used that time to go full throttle with the construction of the projects. He said he had experienced this as IWT commissioner during the dispute over the Baglihar dam, when India would continually urge bilateral talks.

Asked about this, a former official of India's Ministry of Water Resources said India urged bilateral talks because that was the procedure laid down in the IWT.

Political Deadlock

Both sets of officials felt that without political will at the top, transboundary water disputes between India and Pakistan could not be resolved by hydrologists and bureaucrats.

As for the Ratle project on the Chenab, in Doda district of Jammu and Kashmir, Pakistani officials have said that if India goes ahead with the current design, water flow can potentially be reduced by as much as 40%. The dam has been designed to hold

24 million cubic metres of water, while Pakistan wants this to be reduced to 8 million cubic metres.

Asked about this, the former official of India's water resources ministry said the ability to hold back more water was a precaution necessary to minimise the possibility of flash floods that would affect Pakistan the most. He added that there was no reason to fear "the project operator will go against all the norms of a run-of-the-river project and hold back the water, especially when that will mean it will not be able to generate electricity and make money."

But the Pakistani government is not convinced and has already hired two US-based law firms—Three Crowns and Williams & Connelly—according to media reports from Islamabad. Both firms are well known in the US for their lobbying prowess.

Danish Mustafa, independent water expert from Pakistan, blamed the "military driven water nationalists for playing politics and posturing to their own disadvantage" for the current deadlock. He held Pakistan's civilian government responsible as well.

> "As water is an integral component of the agriculture sector, its availability is a prerequisite for building sustainable and resilient livelihoods."

Water Scarcity Is a Product of Flawed International Agreements

Cyril Ferrand

In the following viewpoint, Cyril Ferrand describes the lack of water availability in the West Bank and the Gaza Strip, the two regions in which Palestinians hope to establish their homeland. Both regions are under military occupation, which inhibits Palestinians' access to water for agricultural purposes. Ferrand tracks the water shortages to flaws in the Oslo Peace Accords, an interim peace treaty signed in the 1990s. The United Nations has helped alleviate some of the water access issues by funding the building of new cisterns (and the rehabilitation and repair of existing ones) to collect rainwater, which has been an effective and encouraging partial solution. Ferrand is an agronomist and the Head of Office of the Food and Agriculture Organization of the United Nations (FAO) in the West Bank and Gaza Strip.

As you read, consider the following questions:

1. How is water scarcity affecting food production and agriculture in the Palestinian territories?
2. What steps has the United Nations taken to help alleviate the water crisis in the West Bank and the Gaza Strip?
3. What is rainwater harvesting and how is it being used to mitigate the water crisis?

I n the West Bank and Gaza Strip, water scarcity adds pressure to a region already facing immense challenges. Not only is water scarcity driven by natural hazards but it is also a product of international agreements and of current permit regimes that constrain the construction and rehabilitation of wells.

As water is an integral component of the agriculture sector, its availability is a prerequisite for building sustainable and resilient livelihoods.

The West Bank is in a drought-prone region. Lack of available water year-round threatens the livelihoods of thousands of families dependent upon agriculture for their livelihoods. Rain-fed crops and livestock, an indispensable source for the income and food security for many, have been especially affected by these challenges.

According to a comprehensive World Bank report on the Palestinian water sector, the Oslo Accords and their related administration regime were identified as the principle causes of water scarcity in the West Bank and Gaza Strip. In 1995, the Oslo II Accords (an interim peace agreement) divided the West Bank and Gaza Strip into three administrative areas (A, B and C), with varying levels of security and civil responsibility granted to either the Israeli or Palestinian authorities. Area C, which composes roughly 61% of the West Bank, is under both Israeli civil and military control, leaving Palestinians living there subjected to a restrictive zoning and building regime, greatly impacting their access to water.

Today, farming and herding communities here are especially affected by these policies, as without a connection to the formal water network they are largely dependent upon expensive water transported on tanker trucks for their use.

Under these conditions, challenges are substantial. But the Food and Agriculture Organization of the United Nations (FAO) has identified the "low hanging fruit" that can improve the accessibility and management of water resources to enhance agricultural development.

In partnership with the Ministry of Agriculture and the Palestinian Water Authority, FAO has undertaken various interventions, which include:

- increasing water harvesting and storage capacities at the community and household levels;
- ground water well rehabilitation; unit construction;
- provision of technical support to improve water supply and management;
- support to policy development and coordination across the agriculture sector.

These efforts have resulted in a significant amount of water and money saved.

Facilitating climate-smart agriculture through rainwater harvesting activities

Conservative estimates show that for every USD 1 invested in household cistern construction, at least USD 17.5 worth of water is saved. FAO is working in several vulnerable areas in the West Bank that have especially limited access to water networks and suffer from reoccurring periods of drought. By enabling thousands of families to construct their own cisterns, Palestinians are now able to meet their water needs for both domestic and agricultural purposes.

With a reliable and cost-effective water source, beneficiaries are able to establish backyard gardens, which provide fresh produce either for their own consumption or to be sold at market. The cisterns also increase water storage capacity, allowing households to buy water in greater quantities and at significantly cheaper prices per cubic metre than buying water from tanker trucks.

Most herder communities—particularly in the eastern and southern parts of the West Bank—are in areas that can be difficult for tanker trucks to reach. Not surprisingly, many of these communities already have cisterns that are shared by several families, but have not been properly maintained due to access restrictions and declining standards of living.

This lack of maintenance has caused many cisterns to degrade, making access to water a recurrent and serious issue. Therefore, FAO invested in the rehabilitation of rainwater cisterns to improve access to water at the community level. The large storage capacity and subsequently cheaper access to water strongly lowers households' water costs, thus increasing their resilience in these highly vulnerable areas.

To give you an idea of just how economically practical this intervention is, according to FAO estimates, for every USD 1 invested in community cisterns, USD 77 is saved in water costs. Since the actual structures are already in place and only need repairing, rehabilitation of community rainwater cisterns is one of FAO's most cost-effective activities targeting water resource development.

Cistern construction and rehabilitation has created a reliable source of water, saving farmers a significant amount of money. Communities are now less dependant upon social safety nets and have greater access to food.

> *"In some cases, the disruption or contamination of water supply in urban infrastructures and rural area has incited domestic and cross-border violence."*

Water Access Contributes to a Region's Stability

Christopher Tatlock

In the following classic viewpoint, Christopher Tatlock contends that sub-Saharan Africa has already experienced violence and warfare over water issues. The conflict in Darfur, he points out, was sparked by a dispute over water rights. Tatlock describes the factors that make sub-Saharan Africa one of the regions in the world that is most vulnerable to droughts and lack of safe drinking water for its population. There are a variety of solutions that can help, however, including a combination of water treaties between nations and scientific and engineering technologies than can improve the situation. Tatlock has worked for Council on Foreign Relations, Asia Society, Goldman Sachs, and Franklin Templeton.

"Water Stress in Sub-Saharan Africa," by Christopher W. Tatlock, Council on Foreign Relations, August 7, 2006. Reprinted by permission.

As you read, consider the following questions:

1. What conflicts have already taken place over water in sub-Saharan Africa?
2. Why is this region especially prone to water scarcity?
3. What diplomatic and scientific interventions can help alleviate the water crisis in sub-Saharan Africa?

Introduction

Sub-Saharan Africa suffers from chronically overburdened water systems under increasing stress from fast-growing urban areas. Weak governments, corruption, mismanagement of resources, poor long-term investment, and a lack of environmental research and urban infrastructure only exacerbate the problem. In some cases, the disruption or contamination of water supply in urban infrastructures and rural area has incited domestic and cross-border violence. Experts say incorporating water improvements into economic development is necessary to end the severe problems caused by water stress and to improve public health and advance the economic stability of the region.

What is water stress?

Water stress refers to economic, social, or environmental problems caused by unmet water needs. Lack of supply is often caused by contamination, drought, or a disruption in distribution. In an extreme example, when Côte D'Ivoire split four years ago between the rebel-led north and government-ruled south, the conflict led to unpaid water bills, which precipitated a dangerous health threat in the region, increasing the risk of water-born diseases such as cholera. Some analysts believe the disruption of distribution was a political ploy to put pressure on the rebel-led north.

While water stress occurs throughout the world, no region has been more afflicted than sub-Saharan Africa. The crisis in Darfur stems in part from disputes over water: The conflict that led to the crisis arose from tensions between nomadic farming groups who were competing for water and grazing land—both increasingly scarce due to the expanding Sahara Desert. As Mark Giordano of the International Water Management Institute in Colombo Sri Lanka says, "Most water extracted for development in sub-Saharan Africa—drinking water, livestock watering, irrigation—is at least in some sense 'transboundary.'" Because water sources are often cross-border, conflict emerges.

Why is sub-Saharan Africa more vulnerable to water stress than other regions?

Insufficient infrastructure is a major reason. In a January 2006 UN research paper that assessed global progress on water quality, P.B. Anand, an environmental economist at Britain's Bradford Centre for International Development, noted a significant regional disparity in sanitation infrastructure between sub-Saharan Africa and other regions.

Another disparity is evident within the sub-continent: Of the 980 large dams in sub-Saharan Africa, around 589 are in South Africa, whereas Tanzania, a country with nearly the same land mass and population, only has two large dams. Jonathan Lautze of Tufts University says, "If you look at all of Africa, disproportionate quantities of storage are destined for a few countries like South Africa and Egypt. Generalized regional or continental figures may fail to fully reflect how dire the situation really is in many countries and how much potential for development there is." The UN Environment Program (UNEP) compares water scarcity and quality today with a projection for the future: Currently, access to safe water in sub-Saharan Africa is worse than any other area on the continent, with only 22 percent to 34 percent of populations in at least eight sub-Saharan countries having access to safe water. The UNEP projects that in the year 2025, as many as twenty-five African nations—roughly half the continent's countries—are expected to suffer from a greater combination of increased water scarcity and water stress.

Where are water problems most acute?

Southern-Africa and northern sub-Saharan Africa, in particular the strip across the continent along and north of the Sahel region in West Africa, suffer the most, says Mark Giordano. But Nigeria is also having trouble meeting the UN's Millennium Development Goals (ensure environmental sustainability, combat malaria, improve maternal health, reduce child mortality, eradicate extreme poverty and hunger, etc. by the year 2015) because numerous water projects in the country have been abandoned; high levels of pollution are contaminating available surface water that is abundant but undrinkable. And despite substantial revenue from energy reserves, Ethiopia, Angola, and Niger also suffer from water stress.

Do national boundaries affect water stress?

Yes. When colonial boundaries were drawn, residents were separated from resources, especially water. As Lautze and Giordano discuss in this 2005 *Natural Resources Journal* article, with the manifestation of colonialism emerged the concept of the nation-state, and national boundaries were drawn creating transboundary waters as a byproduct. For example, the Niger basin became transboundary in the colonial period because both the French and Bristish empires shared the water resources, whereas the Senegal river basin was solely under French colonial rule until Guinea gained independence in 1958, which internationalized access to the Senegal river basin.

How do transnational water laws affect water stress?

Giordano believes that transboundary water laws contribute to a history of conflict and resolution in sub-Saharan Africa; "There are still agreements in place which emanated from earlier governments (colonial or minority rule)," he says, "which could be argued to exacerbate tensions between states." Possible examples of agreements which might be argued to have fostered later conflict include those in the Nile Basin (1929 and 1959) and between South Africa and Lesotho (1986). The 1959 Nile Basin agreement preserved British colonial interests in Sudan after Egyptian independence in 1922 and declaration of the Egyptian Republic in 1953, but Egypt and Sudan are the only actors with power in the allocation of Nile resources. The agreement neglects the role of Ethiopia, Tanzania, Uganda, and Rwanda in the governance of transboundary Nile resources.

Successful transboundary water laws have historically been multilateral and focus on joint management and development of resources. Bilateral agreements—such as those in the Nile, Orange, and Inkomati river basins—have proved to be less effective solutions because they focus on water allocation and how to divide limited flows. Allocation is a process of dividing water supplies as opposed to developing and maintaining sustainable water resources for future use. Historically, multilateral agreements further development of sustainable water resources: Such laws govern the Lake Chad, Niger, Okavango, Senegal, and Volta basins and include most or all riparian states (of, on, or relating to the banks of a natural course of water) with the intention of promoting economic development through investment to reduce economic water scarcity.

Experts say that regardless of a country's water abundance or scarcity, development is the only means to ease future water stress. According to Lautze, it was easier for him to take a long shower (water flowed well all the time) in South Africa than Ethiopia, even though Ethiopia is one of the most water-abundant countries in Africa and South Africa is one of the water-poorest. "Differences in natural water endowments may not be the major issue," Lautze says. "This presence or absence of water development can be considered to affect water stress [rather] than natural constraints in sub-Saharan Africa."

What is the relationship between water stress and economic development?

Experts say improving water and sanitation programs is crucial to spurring growth and sustaining economic development. Because it takes time to develop these programs, a paradox emerges: Poor economies are unable to develop because of water stress, and economic instability prohibits the development of programs to abate water stress. A 2005 report commissioned by the governments of Norway and Sweden says that in Kenya, the 1999-2000 drought produced a 16 percent decline in gross domestic product (GDP). Developments in water storage could have prevented that drought from significantly affecting Kenya's economy. Hydropower can also spark economic development. According to Giordano, "Some [transboundary water agreements] also play a clear role in fostering development, for example, by facilitating investment in hydropower and irrigation."

What is the role of agriculture in water stress?

Agricultural development has the potential to improve African economies but requires extensive water supplies. These statistics from the Water Systems Analysis Group at the Institute for the Study of Earth, Oceans, and Space at the University of New Hampshire reveal the urgent need for sustainable agricultural development:

- About 64 percent of Africans rely on water that is limited and highly variable;
- Croplands inhabit the driest regions of Africa where some 40 percent of the irrigated land is unsustainable;
- Roughly 25 percent of Africa's population suffers from water stress;
- Nearly 13 percent of the population in Africa experiences drought-related stress once each generation.

Another aspect of water-related stress is the relationship between water, soil, and agriculture. Pedro Sanchez of the Earth Institute at Columbia University says 96 percent of agriculture in

Africa is rain-fed, but soil nutrient depletion is a more pressing problem than drought in sub-Saharan Africa. Development of soil nutrients as opposed to only allocation of water resources to supply agricultural production is the most effective means to relieve agricultural water stress in the long-term, Sanchez says.

What is the impact of water stress on public health?

Experts say that regions that suffer from water stress serve as catalysts for the spread of disease. In a global study conducted by the United Nations, unsafe water is responsible for around 80 percent of diseases and 30 percent of deaths in developing countries throughout the world. In Africa, which accounts for 90 percent of global cases of malaria, water stress plays an indirect role in curing malaria because it impedes the human recovery process. *The New York Times* recently reported that Angola, despite heavy foreign investment in its oil sector, is enduring a cholera epidemic among its poor linked to shoddy water quality and sanitation.

What can be done to help alleviate water stress in Africa?

Improved access to quality water is a long-term goal that requires more than humanitarian funds.

- Because sub-Saharan Africa is subject to more extreme climate variability than other regions, it needs improved water storage capacity. Some experts say that large dam projects would create a more sustainable reserve of water resources to combat the burden of climate fluctuations, but other disagree, stating the harmful environmental impact of large dams.
- Many experts say more water treaties are needed. Lautze says that transboundary water agreements have cultivated international cooperation and reduced the "probability of conflict and its intensity."

- Better donor emphasis on water development is needed. Giordano is concerned that global environmental issues are upstaging Africa-specific issues of water development.
- Small-scale agricultural improvements also offer a solution to water stress, including the harvest of water in shallow wells, drip irrigation for crops, the use of pumps, and other technological innovations. Sanchez says, "The key thing is the concept of green water as opposed to blue water. Blue water is the water we see in streams. Green water is the water we don't see in the soil, and green water accounts for two-thirds of the water supply." Farmers can access green water through drip irrigation (systems that slowly and consistantly deliver water to plant's toot system), supplemental irrigation (supplementary to natural rainfall rather than the primary source of moisture during periods of drought) and rainwater harvesting (the collection of rainwater for crops, which reduces reliance on irrigation). Crops can grow poorly even during periods of rainfall, and most farms in Africa suffer from nitrogen and phosphorus depletion in soil. One way to assuage water stress in terms of food scarcity is to increase water-holding capacity with organic fertilizers that would increase availability and efficacy of green water.

Periodical and Internet Sources Bibliography

The following articles have been selected to supplement the diverse views presented in this chapter.

Al Jazeera, "Middle East: The Politics of Water," December 11, 2013. http://www.aljazeera.com/programmes/insidestory/2013/12/middle-east-politics-water-2013121183047111535.html

Charis Chang, "Why Everyone Suddenly Has a Thirst for Water," News.com.au, September 18, 2015. http://www.news.com.au/technology/environment/conservation/why-everyone-suddenly-has-a-thirst-for-water/news-story/0a2ff10c8914f47b68fb513ecf8f743c

Lisdey Espinoza Pedraza and Markus Heinrich, "Water Scarcity: Cooperation or Conflict in the Middle East and North Africa?" Foreign Policy Journal, September 2, 2016. http://www.foreignpolicyjournal.com/2016/09/02/water-scarcity-cooperation-or-conflict-in-the-middle-east-and-north-africa/

Anya Groner, "The Politics of Drinking Water," The Atlantic, December 30, 2014. http://www.theatlantic.com/technology/archive/2014/12/the-politics-of-drinking-water/384081/

Navin Singh Khadka, "Are India and Pakistan Set for Water Wars?" BBC, December 22, 2016. http://www.bbc.com/news/world-asia-37521897

Scott Moore, "India's Water Politics: When Drought Leads to Discord," Foreign Affairs, May 29, 2016. https://www.foreignaffairs.com/articles/india/2016-05-29/indias-water-politics

Muhammad Akbar Notezai, "The India-Pakistan Water Dispute," The Diplomat, November 21, 2014. http://thediplomat.com/2014/11/interview-the-india-pakistan-water-dispute/

Te-Ping Chen, "China's Water Problems Are Even Worse Than You Think," Wall Street Journal, January 13, 2015. http://thediplomat.com/2014/11/interview-the-india-pakistan-water-dispute/

David Tickner, "The Silent Crisis: Global Water Scarcity Reshaping Future Foreign Policy," Foreign Policy Centre. http://fpc.org.uk/articles/481

OPPOSING
VIEWPOINTS®
SERIES

CHAPTER 4

What Is the Solution for Reducing Water Scarcity?

Chapter Preface

What is the solution to solving the national and global problem of water scarcity? Some scientists and water experts don't think there even is one—the only path forward, they say, will be focused on conserving and managing what little resources are left.

In the United States alone, a majority of states have reported experiencing "water stress," which is a situation in which water demands exceed the available amount for a certain period of time. It can also refer to regions in which water is available but contaminated and therefore not safe for human consumption or agricultural use. As a result, many organizations and government agencies have emphasized water conservation efforts: that is, they have outlined practical ways to stop water waste and pollution. For example, they recommend using plants that don't require much watering in landscaping designs, as well as household tricks such as taking shorter showers and cleaning outdoor areas with a broom rather than hosing them down with water.

Water conservation is a worthwhile endeavor, and it reminds us of the ways in which people can use water more efficiently. Others have not given up, however, on a "solution" to the water crisis. They argue that there are many viable ways to alleviate the current conditions, and they involve a multitude of fields: political negotiations, engineering improvements to infrastructure, and desalination methods, among others.

One interesting solution is the desalination of water, in which ocean and seawater is filtered to remove the salt, thus rendering it drinkable and safe. But does desalination pose another kind of threat to the environment altogether?

Still another solution involves irrigation innovations, to produce "more crop per drop" of water. There is also one solution that many are saying is the only one: limiting human population growth, so that there is enough water to sustain the needs of everyone on the planet. But can irrigation improvements make a significant difference?

This chapter offers viewpoints that highlight many of these solutions, with a special focus on what China, which has one of the world's largest populations, is doing to apply innovative remedies to the crisis. The challenge of water scarcity is certainly frightening, but human ingenuity and cooperation might be the answer.

> *"Although we live on a planet that is covered with water, very little of that is fresh: in fact, if all of the world's water could fit into a gallon jug, the freshwater available for our use would equal only about one tablespoon."*

Stop Population Growth to End Water Scarcity

Laurie Mazur

In the following viewpoint, Laurie Mazur argues that water scarcity is a problem with a straightforward solution: limit population growth. In the regions of the world where water is most scarce, she writes, human population is growing, rather than shrinking, which is making the problem of water stress even worse. Water scarcity, she explains, has another, related problem: the lack of availability of safe drinking water. Overpopulated areas are unable to maintain the proper infrastructure to deliver clean, drinkable water to their inhabitants. Contaminated water leads to an increase in disease and public health risk. Mazur is a consultant on population and the environment for the Wilson Center's Environmental Change and Security Program and the urban resilience editor for Island Press, which publishes expert writing on environmental issues.

"Water and Population: Limits to Growth?" appears courtesy of Laurie Mazur and New Security Beat, which is published by the Wilson Center's Environmental Change and Security Program. www.wilsoncenter.org/ecsp and www.newsecuritybeat.org, February 3, 2012. Reprinted by permission.

As you read, consider the following questions:

1. What are the two components of the water crisis, according to Mazur?
2. What are the measures that can be taken to alleviate water scarcity?
3. How are poor people more susceptible to problems related to water scarcity?

Water—essential, finite, and increasingly scarce—has been dubbed "the new oil." Experts debate whether human societies are approaching "peak water," beyond which lies a bleak future of diminishing supplies and soaring demand. Others observe that, for many, the water crisis has already arrived.

Indeed, if any resource poses a serious limit to growth on human numbers and appetites, it would have to be water. The planet's supply of freshwater is fixed, and there is no substitute for its life-giving qualities.

Still, a general water crisis is not inevitable. It is true that people are placing unsupportable stress on freshwater supplies in many areas, while climate change threatens the quantity and reliability of those supplies. And population dynamics, especially growth and migration, contribute to the problem in ways both obvious and less so. However, a broad range of supply- and demand-side solutions are available and implementing those solutions could relieve—and avert—tremendous human suffering.

The "water crisis," as reported in the media, is actually two oft-conflated crises. First, there is the physical scarcity of water, experienced in arid areas from Yemen to the American Southwest. Second, there is the shortage of safe drinking water, typically caused by a lack of infrastructure in poor countries—even those with plenty of rainfall, such as Uganda. Some regions—notably the Horn of Africa—struggle with both crises at once.

Assessing Scarcity

Physical scarcity of water is a significant and growing problem. Although we live on a planet that is covered with water, very little of that is fresh: in fact, if all of the world's water could fit into a gallon jug, the freshwater available for our use would equal only about one tablespoon. In addition, that tiny sip of water is distributed very inequitably. So, while there is no global shortage, a growing number of regions are chronically parched.

Today, about one third of the world's population lives in countries with moderate to high water stress; by 2025, largely because of population growth, fully two out of three of the world's people will live under those conditions. A recent McKinsey and Company report warns that within two decades, demand for water will exceed supply by 40 percent.

Human numbers are growing most rapidly where water is scarce. The World Bank's *Water and Development* report identified 45 "water poor" countries that are both physically short on water and economically impoverished. Those countries have an average fertility rate of 4.8 children per woman—nearly twice the world average—and their populations are expected to double by 2050. "Rapid population growth makes water problems more complicated and difficult to solve," said Sandra Postel, director of the Global Water Policy Project, in an interview.

When water-stressed countries lack surface water supplies, they typically resort to overpumping underground aquifers, drawing down wells faster than they can be replenished. As a result, groundwater levels have dropped precipitously in many places over the past nine years, and wells have gone dry in parts of India, China, and Pakistan.

The depletion of groundwater is an ominous sign for world food production, which must increase 70 percent by 2050 to meet the demands of a growing world population. Postel estimates that 10 percent of world food production now depends on the overpumping of groundwater.

And then there is the wild card of climate change, which has already begun to disrupt rainfall patterns and intensify drought in many parts of the world. The famine ravaging the Horn of Africa may be a harbinger of what is to come for fragile nations. Many countries, including Kenya and Ethiopia, are likely to experience longer, harsher droughts, which—superimposed on existing water scarcity, rapid population growth, poor governance, and poverty—could create the conditions for widespread starvation and misery.

In another grim development, climate change is melting glaciers and snowpack on the world's great mountain ranges, including the Himalayas, Hindu Kush, and Andes, which supply drinking water for one in six of the world's people. New evidence shows that those glaciers are disappearing faster than expected, leading to water shortages in Peru and elsewhere.

Quality and Delivery

The other water crisis—the shortage of clean drinking water—is not simply about the physical scarcity of water. Nor is it simply about poverty, though more funds are needed to address the problem.

Today, nearly a billion people lack access to clean drinking water; 2.5 billion lack adequate sanitation; and some 5 million die every year due to preventable water-related diseases.

Nowhere is the crisis more evident than in the fast-expanding cities of the developing world. Cities have seen explosive growth in recent decades, and the UN predicts that by midcentury the world's urban population will nearly double, from 3.5 to 6.3 billion – an increase equivalent to the current population of China, India, and the United States combined. Developing regions as a whole will account for 93 percent of that growth; more than 80 percent will be in the cities of Asia and Africa.

It is safe to say that they are not ready. Most of those cities are already failing to provide basic services—including water and sanitation—to new arrivals, who typically occupy informal slums and shanty towns beyond the reach of municipal services.

For example, Dhaka has grown sixfold since 1975 and is now home to nearly 17 million people but has "water supply network coverage for only a small fraction of this population," according to Pier Mantovani, lead water supply and sanitation specialist at the World Bank. As a result, in areas not served by official services, including the city's slums, people pay exorbitant prices to middlemen with tankers selling water of dubious quality.

Here, too, population dynamics play a role. Migration, mostly from rural areas, accounts for roughly 40 percent of urban growth. That migration is spurred, in part, by rapid growth in the countryside, where the total fertility rate (average number of children born per woman) is usually higher. The remaining 60 percent of urban growth results from "natural increase," meaning simply that there are more births than deaths. Population growth, then, is a driving force behind the breakneck pace of urbanization and compounds the challenges of providing safe water to city dwellers.

Silver Linings

Today's twin water crises pose enormous challenges for human well-being and even survival. Without a dramatic change of course, water could indeed pose a severe "limit to growth" of the human enterprise. As Margaret Catley-Carlson, vice-chair of the World Economic Forum Global Agenda Council on water security, has written:

> [I]f "business as usual" water management practices continue for another two decades, large parts of the world will face a serious and structural threat to economic growth, human well-being, and national security.

But there are alternatives to "business as usual."

Consider this: despite its growing scarcity, vast amounts of water are wasted through inefficiency; growing water-intensive crops in dry areas or using drinking water for purposes (like flushing toilets) where non-potable "grey" water would suffice, for example. Such waste is a "silver lining," said Postel. By reducing waste, "we can get the most value from limited water supplies."

Rethinking pricing is key. Irrigation is heavily subsidized in many parts of the world; farmers typically pay just 15 to 20 percent of the cost of the water they use, according to Postel. Reducing those generous subsidies would make conservation more cost-effective.

Meeting the need for safe drinking water will require greater attention to the needs of the poor, especially in informal urban settlements. That, in turn, will require a mobilization of resources and political will. "In every country," said Mantovani, "politicians swear that 'water is life,' and that providing safe drinking water is a critically important policy priority…but in many countries water supply is not adequately funded or supported."

On the demand side, slower population growth would help reduce pressure on limited water supplies, providing some breathing room to develop creative solutions. As it happens, many water-poor countries also have high levels of "unmet need" for family planning—they are home to millions of women who want to prevent or postpone getting pregnant but aren't using modern contraception. Investments in family planning programs could improve women's health and well-being, slow population growth, and reduce vulnerability to water stress.

In short, solutions abound. "We can meet the water needs of seven billion and have healthy aquatic ecosystems at the same time," said Postel. However, she added, "We are not moving toward those solutions at a rate commensurate with the problem."

"Humans have always looked to nature for inspiration to solve problems."

Learn Nature's Lessons for Water Conservation

Stephanie Vierra

In the following viewpoint, Stephanie Vierra contends that nature has always inspired human ingenuity. Just as human flight was inspired by the biological structure of birds, so too can other elements and "designs" within nature serve to influence the ways in which humans approach problem solving. One of Vierra's examples describes the way in which The Thorny Devil, a lizard whose habitat is the desert, supplies itself with hydration by absorbing it from the environment. Studying its method of collecting moisture might serve to inspire an innovation that could help alleviate water scarcity. Vierra is the president and owner of Vierra Design & Education Services, LLC, specializing in research, project management, and educational programs on sustainability and whole building design.

"Biomimicry: Designing to Model Nature," by Stephanie Vierra, Whole Building Design Guide and National Institute of Building Science, October 23, 2014. Reprinted by permission.

As you read, consider the following questions:

1. What is biomimicry?
2. What are some of the most successful examples of human innovation that have been inspired by biomimicry?
3. How does The Thorny Devil collect water, and how can it influence scientific technology for human benefit?

Introduction

The Biomimicry Institute defines biomimicry as the science and art of emulating Nature's best biological ideas to solve human problems. For billions of years nature—animals, plants, and even microbes—has been solving many of the problems we are still dealing with today. Each has found what works, what is appropriate, and what lasts.

Biomimicry and biomimetics come from the Greek words bios, meaning life, and mimesis, also meaning to imitate. Scientist and author Janine Benyus popularized the term biomimicry in her 1997 book *Biomimicry: Innovation Inspired by Nature.* Benyus believes that most of the problems that have ever existed have already been solved by nature. Benyus suggests shifting one's perspective from learning about nature to learning from nature as a way to solve human problems. Sustainability issues are among those that can be addressed by applying the biomimicry process to a project. Utilizing an integrated design process can help open up opportunities to identify biological solutions to building problems and include the perspective of nature in the design process—as it is likely that nature already offers a solution.

Description

Humans have always looked to nature for inspiration to solve problems. Leonardo da Vinci applied biomimicry to the study of birds in the hope of enabling human flight. He very closely observed the anatomy and flight of birds, and made numerous notes and sketches of his observations and countless sketches of proposed "flying machines". Although he was not successful with his own flying machine, his ideas lived on and were the source of inspiration for the Wright Brothers, who were also inspired by their observations of pigeons in flight. They finally did succeed in creating and flying the first airplane in 1903.

Recent success stories exist in terms of how biomimicry can be applied to building design. While buildings serve to protect us from nature's extremes, this does not mean that they do not have anything to learn from the biological world. In fact, nature regularly builds structures with functionality that human-built structures could usefully emulate. Biomimetic research, science, and applications continue to grow and are already influencing the next generation of building products and systems as well as whole building designs.

For example, photovoltaic systems, which harvest solar energy, are a first step at mimicking the way a leaf harvests energy. Research is underway to create solar cells that more closely resemble nature. These cells are water-gel-based—essentially artificial leaves—that couple plant chlorophyll with carbon materials, ultimately resulting in a more flexible and cost-effective solar cell.

The bumpy surface of a lotus leaf acts as a self-cleaning mechanism allowing dirt to be cleansed off the surface naturally by water, for instance, during a rain shower. Even the smallest of breezes on the plant causes a subtle shift in the angle of the plant allowing gravity to remove the dirt without the plant having to expend any energy. This same idea has been applied to the design of new building materials such as paints, tiles, textiles, and glass that reduce the need for detergents and labor and also reduces maintenance and material replacement costs.

Researchers have also developed non-toxic, formaldehyde-free wood glue that is now used in hardwood, plywood, and particleboard projects. The researchers discovered how to do this by understanding how blue mussels attach firmly under the water using flexible, thread-like tentacles.

The Thorny Devil, a desert lizard, gathers all the water it needs directly from rain, standing water, or from soil moisture, against gravity without using energy or a pumping device. Water is conveyed to the lizard's mouth by capillary action through a circulatory system on the surface of its skin. This same concept could be applied to passive collection and distribution systems of naturally distilled water which would reduce the energy consumed in collecting and transporting water by pump action (e.g., to the tops of buildings), and provide other inexpensive technological solutions such as managing heat through evaporative cooling systems, and protecting structures from fire through on-demand water barriers.

Damage to an organism naturally elicits a healing response. Bone is also known to detect damage to itself and can heal within range of its initial strength. This same concept has been applied to synthetic material design and contributed to the development of a self-healing polymer for use as building materials. Tiny capsules containing a healing agent are embedded in the polymer. When the material is damaged, the capsules rupture and release the healing agent, which repairs the cracks. The self-repairing capabilities of materials can contribute to reduced maintenance and material replacements costs as well as increased durability. Self-repairing materials can also be made lighter, resulting in reduced embodied energy and greenhouse gas production.

[…]

| "Nature has been providing
desalination services ever since water
has been on the planet."

We Should Learn to Replicate Natural Desalination

Aditya Sood

In the following viewpoint, Aditya Sood suggests that we look to nature to help solve problems of water scarcity. Nature already has found ways to desalinate water, Sood argues. The sun's heat causes water from the oceans to evaporate, salt-free, and that water is then carried by clouds and redistributed over land. If scientists can find ways to replicate this cycle, Sood writes, then water scarcity may be solved on a global scale. This excerpted article discusses the practical issues in making this vision a reality, including funding the technology and harnessing the renewable energy that would be required. Sood is a researcher on integrated hydrological modeling at the International Water Management Headquarters in Sri Lanka.

As you read, consider the following questions:

1. What is nature's method of desalinating water?
2. What are some of the constraints on making desalination a practical solution?
3. If the energy becomes available, how soon could desalination become a viable option?

The famous quote, "Water, water, everywhere, nor any drop to drink," may become a quote of past, at least for the coastal cities, if desalination by renewable energy takes off. Desalination is a process that removes salt and other minerals from saline water. It is becoming an increasingly popular technology as it can ease water scarcity in urban areas and free up water for the environmental flow regulations, while also reducing pressure on agriculture.

Nature has been providing desalination services ever since water has been on the planet. The sun provides unlimited energy to evaporate water out of sea; clouds with the aid of wind distribute the fresh water over large stretches of land. The freshwater eventually comes back to the sea, thus maintaining the salt concentration in the oceans. Can humans replicate this natural cycle?

The Current State of Desalination

Desalination by humans has been practiced for hundreds of years, although at commercial scale it only picked up since the mid-1970s. From a mere global capacity of less than 1 million m3/day in 1970s, it has progressed to over 70 million m3/day capacity in 2012. This looks impressive, except most of the desalination is concentrated in a few countries. Its development has only taken place in either energy rich regions (i.e. where energy is very cheap) or affluent nations. Energy cost forms a large component of costs of desalination – up to 45% of the operative cost, which is the constraining factor in the widespread use of desalination.

Currently the top 3 countries in desalination are Saudi Arabia, USA and UAE. The Middle East and Northern African region of

DESALINATION IS EXPENSIVE AND DAMAGING TO THE ENVIRONMENT

A report by Lux Research indicates that to meet the demands of a growing human population, worldwide desalinated water supply must triple by 2020. This report indicates that desalination is feasible, as the global water desalination market is expected to expand at a compound annual growth rate of 9.5 percent over the next 10 years.

While desalination is garnering considerable interest, it is not price competitive with traditional water sources. The construction, operation and maintenance costs make desalination at least three times as expensive as traditional sources.

In addition to its high cost, desalination technologies are harmful to the environment. Removing salt from seawater produces brine, which contains twice the salt of seawater; they also contain contaminants that can affect marine life when dumped back to the sea. If brine is disposed on land, it could seep through the soil and pollute water reserves underground.

The US Environmental Protection Agency found that desalination plants kill at least 3.4 billion fish and other marine life annually. This represents a $212.5 million loss to commercial fisheries. Desalination plants can also destroy up to 90 percent of plankton and fish eggs in the surrounding water.

Water recycling is a means of purifying water so that it can be made potable. However, as with desalination, there are problems with this approach including the amount of energy needed to power wastewater recycling.

According to the National Research Council, the redistribution of water can be more efficient and cheaper than desalination. Numerous studies support the council's report; they indicate that management alternatives and efficiency programs can reduce water supply problems at a much lower cost, without the environmental and health dangers associated with large-scale desalination plants.

"Is Desalination a Solution to the World Water Crisis?" by Richard Matthews, Global Warming Is Real, March 23, 2011. Licensed under CC BY-SA 3.0.

the world (where energy is abundant), accounts for 38% of the global capacity. In spite of high energy costs, the desalination cost has come down substantially over the last four decades. In terms of 2010 USD, the cost of desalination has fallen from USD 9/m3 in 1970 to about USD 0.5/m3. This can be attributed to improvements in desalination technology and increases in the scale of operations. This is still too high for many regions of the world (for example, based on data collected by GWI from 180 cities around the world, the average water tariff per cubic meter of water in 2010 USD for different regions are: sub-Saharan Africa, $ 0.09; south Asia, $ 0.08; Eastern Europe and Central Asia, $ 0.28; Latin America, $ 0.41).

Can Renewable Energy Save the Day?

As the energy prices rise, desalination might seem out of reach but can renewable energy save the day? As of now there is very small renewable energy based desalination capacity (about 1% of the total desalination capacity) but the cost of producing water using renewable energy is very high – almost 3 to 8 times of that from conventional energy. Renewable energy technology such as photovoltaic (PV) is relatively new and the cost of such technology is falling rapidly. In 2010 USD, the cost of PV module has fallen from about $70/W in 1975 to less than $2/W in 2010.

Two trends give hope for the future. First, the current data shows that with the increasing per capita GDP, people pay higher tariffs for water. Second, both, the desalination technology and renewable (in this case PV) technology are still developing and have a much greater scope for price reduction.

In a study conducted at IWMI, we looked at the historic trends and developed relationships between production and cost of production for desalination (without the energy component). In the research, the world was divided into 7 regions. Based on projected per capita GDP, we projected the water tariffs that people would be willing to pay in each region. Using the existing relationships (from literature) developed for PV, along with the relationships developed for desalination, we tried to find out at what global production level of each technology would it be viable to use desalination by renewable energy to meet the people's water demand at their willingness to pay rates, within 100 km of the coast.

If energy is not a constraint, desalination will become a viable option by 2040 in most of the regions of the world. Sub Saharan Africa and South Asia, where water tariffs are low, require about 32 and 56 million m3/day capacity development each year till 2050 to be viable. This has to be seen in the context that the current global production of desalination is 70 million m3/day. Even with PV energy, desalination is feasible with minimal growth in most of the regions of the world (less than 1 million MW new capacity each year). For feasibility in Sub Saharan Africa and South Asia, growth of roughly 170 and 350 MW/year new production is required. Since 1992, the PV production has grown at a rate of 2.2 GW/year.

But desalination does not come without environmental costs. Disposing brine and other chemicals used in the desalination process can be environmentally harmful. When looking at greater scales of desalination expansion, the environmental costs of desalination needs to be considered, although we did not address them in this analysis.

Will desalination become a viable option by 2040 in Sub Saharan Africa and South Asia? This will depend on the market forces and government policies. The incentive to invest in desalination will likely increase as renewable energy prices decline and as countries experience increasing pressure from water scarcity.

> *"The incremental water supply
> from the project would help the
> receiving region keep pace with the
> development of the entire country."*

Technology and Engineering Can Fix Water Scarcity in China

Yu Yang, Lei Yin, and Qingzong Zhang

China has embarked on a fascinating technological and engineering solution of two of its major problems: the southern region is prone to flooding, while the northern region is facing a water shortage. The South-to-North Water Diversion Project is an attempt to transfer water from the flooded region to be used in the north. In the following excerpted viewpoint, the authors consider the project and its implications and chances for success. Yu Yang is in the Department of Public Administration of China's Southeast University. Qingzong Zhang is at the School of Economics and Management at China's Southeast University.

"Quantity versus Quality in China's South-to-North Water Diversion Project: A System Dynamics Analysis", by Yu Yang, Lei Yin and Qingzong Zhang, MDPI AG, May 11, 2015. http://www.mdpi.com/2073-4441/7/5/2142/htm. Licensed under CC BY 4.0 International.

As you read, consider the following questions:

1. What is the South-to-North Water Diversion (SNWD) Project?
2. What problems could the project be facing in terms of water quality and quantity?
3. What is more crucial, according to the authors: quantity or quality?

Introduction

The South-to-North Water Diversion (SNWD) Project (official translation), or the South-to-North Water Transfer Project, is an infrastructure project designed to divert water from flood-prone southern rivers to China's water-poor northern region [1]. According to the project plan, the annual volume of diverted water is 44.8 billion cubic meters. The size is close to the total water volume of China's Yellow River, which is the third longest river in Asia [2]. Although approximately 253 billion Yuan (Chinese currency, 1 Yuan = 0.16 U.S. dollar) has been invested in its construction [3], from a cost-benefit point of view, the SNWD Project is a feasible choice for North China and the rest of the country [4,5]. A study on water vulnerability and demand-supply balance dynamics indicates that the incremental water supply from the project would help the receiving region keep pace with the development of the entire country [6].

Similarly to other mega-projects in China and worldwide [7,8], however, controversies surrounding the SNWD Project have continuously been debated by numerous stakeholders and researchers [9,10,11]. Technological, economic, social, ecological and even political disputes are constant [12]. One-third of the provinces in China are included in the project, and over 200 million people would benefit from the water diversion, making the endeavor more than a simple infrastructure project. To ensure that the project better serves households, firms and farmers, among the disputes, the central concern should focus on the basic demands of those affected. Water demands can be interpreted from two perspectives: efficiently tackling the increasing water gap for human water users and effectively meeting drinking and nondrinking water requirements. Finally, a sustainable water management pattern that not only guarantees a sufficient amount of water but also satisfies a certain standard of water quality should be achieved. Thus, a water transfer project should attain water quantity and water quality goals simultaneously, which is the primary focus of this article.

With decades of studies on the planning and construction of the SNWD Project, the amounts of diverted water and related effects have been well addressed [13,14]. Nonetheless, for a project that virtually violates the laws of nature, the indirect effects of the water diversion have yet to be fully discussed. At the pre-construction stage, some scholars and experts took interest in the environmental uncertainties associated with the project [15,16]. Moreover, cooperation among regions has been obstructed by the activities of the primary polluters [17]. Some authors have proposed that the ultimate objective of the SNWD Project is to improve the water environment rather than meet the water demand gap [12]. The costs of the SNWD Project include furthering environmental deterioration through rapid rural transition [18]. Evidence from virtual water calculations shows that North China exports over 50 billion m3 of virtual water (amounting to over one-third of the supply) to South China annually. A majority of the virtual water flow occurs in the form of agriculture products, and brings stress for the water-exporting provinces. [19,20]. Thus, diverted high-quality water is critical for the receiving region as well as the supplier, which is the actual receiver of the "water". In December 2014, President Xi Jinping urged stronger management to protect water quality and conserve water [21]. With the SNWD Project entering the formal operational phase, controversies should be analyzed from a dynamic perspective. In this paper, therefore, we consider the future and investigate the intrinsic link between water quantity and water quality during the upcoming operational stage instead of studying water quantity during the pre-construction and construction stage, as has been done in the existing literature.

Regarding the dilemma of quantity and quality in the SNWD Project, we must provide answers to certain unanswered questions. Which is comparatively more essential, water quantity or water quality? Would an emphasis on water pollution treatment introduce extra costs and offset growth in certain regions? To gain better knowledge on potential outcomes, the research community has sought to apply mathematical models in the analysis. Typical quantitative decision-making tools and the computable general equilibrium model have been employed [6,22,23]. Using established simulation methods, data output under various conditions have been obtained to provide information for comparison and further policy design. In most previous studies, the two variables, water quantity and water quality, have been treated separately, which is partly a result of the complexity of the economic-social-ecological analytical framework and is also related to the difficulty of the model description. With the goal of systematically characterizing the inherent relationship between water quantity and water quality, this paper utilizes a methodology of system dynamics analysis to investigate the effects and the trends of the SNWD Project and discusses the implications for sustainable development based on the results of the quantity-quality interaction. Furthermore, these findings may contribute to research and policy applications in other similarly marginal environments around the world. The remainder of this paper is structured as follows. We first describe the study area, the modeling method and data sources used. Then, through a well-designed system dynamics model, we analyze the effects of water quantity and quality in various scenarios. The results of the simulation and prediction are then reviewed and further discussed. Finally, we summarize the study and present policy suggestions for sustainable water management.

[...]

Discussions

Trade-Offs in the SNWD Project

The simulations found have provided definite answers to the central question raised in this paper. There is no contradiction between the quantity and quality of diverted water. It is clear that economic and social development in regions with water shortages requires that more water be made available and that the SNWD Project could vastly improve the situation. Furthermore, the quality of transferred water is equally essential to the sustainable growth of the water-receiving areas. Environmental limitations exist in all economic activities, including agriculture and industry, as well as the urban expansion that creates more groundwater funnels. Therefore, the water diversion program should address the economic dimension and also avoid the imminent conflict with the water environment.

The preliminary findings have shown that the water quantity-quality trade-off could obtain a point of equilibrium, while this trade-off is not the only one in the SNWD Project. In the simulations of various subsystems, despite the minor changes in population, another potential trade-off exists between agriculture and industry. This trade-off is essentially a comparison between marginal costs and marginal benefit. As for the agricultural sector, it is related to the safeguarding of the national food security in China [46]. The simple calculation on the water usage and the economic output is not sufficient for the social optimization, especially when its production and yields would decrease due to urbanization [47]. As for the industrial sector, it has contributed the majority in the GDP accumulation, yet with even more pollution and violating social welfare [44]. Therefore, there exists a certain side effect in the water diversion, i.e., the results show no limitation for industrial growth. For the purpose of realizing synergy among economic, social and environmental goals, it is necessary to build a multi-objective coordination model for the SNWD supply system. The trade-off between water resource allocation and quality protection is a fundamental issue. Meanwhile, the full consideration of the production decision-making and related by-products in agricultural, industrial and other sectors is a prerequisite as well. Without this mechanism, there might be some obstructions to achieving the ideal results of water quantity and quality.

The research findings presented above are straightforward, one reason possibly being the study area of focus. We focused on a single province, so that certain other factors could be ignored. If we were to include other provinces, the analysis and simulation model would be more complicated. Because the conflicts and coordination between provincial boundaries are increasingly significant [48], the political dimension factors are difficult to describe in the quantitative model. Furthermore, in this case, we should also consider that the central government would be involved, making the entire conflict hierarchical [49]. Thus the third trade-off between provincial boundaries, or between central and local governments, would make a further renegotiation and possibly change the designed water quantity and quality proposals.

Further Stages under Planning
The SNWD Project has yet to be fully accomplished. The completed project in late-2013 was the first stage of the eastern route. Thus, the quantitative analysis in the sections above was actually based on the conditions and data in that early stage. Findings from the simulation did not take the new project construction into consideration.

When discussing the upcoming second stage that remains in the planning process, a more comprehensive thinking is required. Though some explicit predictions have been achieved, they need to be combined with some other real-world policies. The most considerable one is from the State Council of China. In January 2013, the No. 2013-2 Document "Assessment Methods for the Most Strict Water Resource Management System" was issued. The policy outlines the principles of China's water resource management from a macro perspective. It sets the overall national water consumption on a limitation of 700 billion m³ per year, as well as the control targets for every province. Among them, Jiangsu Province is given a quota restriction of 50.8 billion m3 in 2015, and 52.4 billion m3 in 2020 [50]. The limitation for Shandong Province is 25.1 billion m3 (2015) and 27.7 billion m3 (2020), while for Tianjin, it is 2.8 billion m3 and 3.8 billion m3, respectively. The amount of transferred water is equivalent to nearly 60 percent of Jiangsu's total water supply. It would significantly relieve stresses for the water consumption in both Shandong and Tianjin. However, the water quantity-controlling regime has brought more significant pressure for Jiangsu. Related evidence is the No. 2011-29 Document "The Water Resource Planning in Jiangsu Province" from the Water Resources Department of Jiangsu Province. The planning goal of water usage in 2020 is 59 billion m3 [51]. However, the State Council cut this standard down 6.6 billion m3 two years later in the No. 2013-2 Document.

The solution for this rigorous situation is quite complicated, while the analysis might put forward a workable suggestion. Since the water quality has a specific connection with the water diversion amount, the control of the pollution rate could be the breakthrough point. A reduced pollution level leads to a higher efficiency of water consumption. For example, in 2020, the industrial GDP for the case of TW = 15 and PR = 10% (9403.85 billion) is greater than the case of TW = 30 and PR = 15% (9397.56 billion). If the water quality could be improved in the following years, the targeted water supply goal would not be a problem for Jiangsu. Therefore, the outputs of the first stage are the inputs for the second stage. With an increasing demand in the second stage, it is necessary for water providing regions to establish a clear objective system on water quality upgrading so as to enhance the current usage efficiency and to satisfy the further needs from the northern provinces and even the capital.

Some Neglected Factors

The research on the water quantity-quality interaction has covered several factors including economic, social and ecological dimensions. Meanwhile, the system dynamics model has its unique advantage in describing the effects of water diversion from various perspectives. However, some key influential factors are still missing.

This study has only predicted the case for the time horizon up to the year 2020, which is based on an implicit assumption that no eventful technological or structural change will occur. Thus, all of the results pertain to the current technological conditions. While it is increasingly emphasized in China that local governments put huge efforts into the research and development of techniques with water efficiency and pollution control [52], the results in the next five years would possibly change. In view of this surmise, it could be optimistic about the potential difficulties in further project stages under planning.

The structural characteristics of the various economic sectors have also been considered to remain unchanged. This means that the initial proportion settings in Table 1 are relatively stable during the eight-year simulation period. Most of the graphs indicate exponential growth curves, corresponding to the ongoing and upcoming high-speed growth in China. The growth rate is extraordinarily high for Jiangsu Province, especially for its north and central regions (the cities included in this study), which have annual GDP growth rates over 12 percent and industrial growth rates of nearly 14 percent [53]. However, we could expect that in the long run, more significant technological progresses will occur, with a transformed industrial structure, and the flow and stock of the outcome variables would differ. Currently, the transforming degrees in the agriculture (first) sector are relatively low, since the changes of its share in GDP were less than 0.2 percent in the recent five years. The changes are more clear and satisfying in the industrial (second) sector, with the annual declining rates between one and 1.4 percent [53]. Thus, a transition to an s-shaped curve would occur a few decades later, when the parameters given in this study fundamentally change. This trend will bring a remission to the water consumption pressure, especially for the providing regions. Meanwhile, the central and local governments would definitely push forward the acceleration of economic structural transformation [54]. This is a factor of policy and will be discussed in the next paragraphs.

For a great national infrastructure project, the influence of the policy dimension is crucial, as well. Most of this paper presented an engineering perspective by setting different water transfer and pollution rate levels, which is independent of policy. All of the initial parameters have been partially determined by central or local policies and stabilized after years of evolution. Governments have the ability to co-opt environmental policies to pursue other strategic objectives [55]. As the SNWD Project has completed its construction stage and begun formal operations, the influence from policy-makers, rather than engineers, should be allotted more significance.

There are three priority factors related to policies. The first is the water price mechanism. Although the Jiangsu Water Source Company Ltd., on behalf of the provincial government, is charged with the water market businesses, including water price setting, water is a special product that is a necessity for the basic needs of residents and farmers. Water consumption could not be handled totally under commercial principles. Water-providing areas have complained about the costs they bear as part of the SNWD water treatment and other issues. The central government is requested to impose an "SNWD tax" on beneficiaries of the project [56]. If similar tax or subsidy policies are introduced into the water price mechanism, an ideal condition that makes the marginal costs approximate the marginal revenue could be formed. In an economic view, the efficiency of water usage would increase significantly under a better price mechanism. As a consequence, the results of the water transfer amounts could reduce accordingly.

The second is the water pollution control mechanism. Prior to the operation of the SNWD Project, over 400 pollution prevention projects, with a total investment over 15 billion Yuan, have been implemented in the water quality programs of the eastern route [57]. However, the decentralized regime in China and in this project has weakened local environment agencies, and the pollution fees from firms are often too low [58]. As a national infrastructure project, local officials should receive powerful support from the central governments. With the incentives of the pilot program on Water Ecological Civilization Cities [59], greater efforts in monitoring and detecting water pollution, advocating for responsive policies in local levels will lead to an improvement in water quality. Last, but not least, social participation is substantial. It is critical for both water quantity and water quality. As for the water consumption, policies focusing on social concerns with education programs implemented for water conservation could reduce individual daily water usages. Meanwhile, calling for stronger institutionalized public engagements would create a culture of conservation and provide a strong impetus for addressing water pollution [60].

Furthermore, we only treat the water quantity and quality as exogenous variables. Some endogenous factors, such as biological and chemical ones, are highly relevant to water quality, as well. Future climate conditions that might affect economic (especially agriculture) and environmental indicators are also unknown. Further research on those factors might be helpful to better understanding the findings in this study.

Conclusions and Policy Implications

This study uses the system dynamics method to analyze the interaction between water quantity and water quality in China's SNWD Project. The economic and environmental effects for various scenarios of transferred water and pollution rates are calculated. This research differs from other work in that we choose a specific province, covering both the water-providing and water-receiving areas. Although the system dynamics model and other mathematical tools have been used in other studies in the past, most of those studies have treated the factors of quantity and quality separately. In our model, five subsystems of water, agriculture, industry, population and the environment are included simultaneously, and data from 2002 to 2012 are collected. We develop simulations through the year 2020 to assess water quantity and quality effects and to obtain insight into sustainable water management in the related areas.

Based on the simulation results obtained for the economic and environmental indicators at the different levels of water quantity and water quality, certain conclusions can be drawn. First, the SNWD Project could provide a sufficient quantity of water for economic growth in the receiving regions. Second, an efficient quantity of transferred water exists, which demonstrates the growth limitation for both agriculture and the groundwater funnel. Third, upgrades in water quality could mutually reinforce the quantity effect and greatly promote economic growth, as well. Environmental limitation exists in all economic activities. Therefore, from a general perspective, both water quantity and water quality are equally crucial in the SNWD Project. The water diversion project is not only intended to reduce water constraints; it is also an opportunity to promote sustainable development and the establishment of an ecologically conscious civilization [61]. These findings also provide certain policy implications for the government and the public.

The source of the SNWD eastern route is the Yangtze River, the longest in Asia and the third longest in the world, and its downstream could provide almost a limitless water supply. This study shows that although the water source has no natural limitation, the use of it has environmental limitations for all economic activities. Therefore, an essential policy recommendation is that the operational stage of the SNWD Project requires a transition from efficient water diversion to effective water diversion. This means greater priority should be given to providing a sufficient amount of drinking and nondrinking water of high quality, rather than simply satisfying the water shortage with a specific amount of water. In practice, local governments also face the dilemma of low water prices and high water use efficiency, with the aim of satisfying economic needs, as well as environmental objectives [62]. Thus, certain regulations should be employed. Typical policy choices for some local governments include economic incentives, such as water quality permit trading or the use of environmental taxes (e.g., the "SNWD tax"). The central government needs to launch a water-quality-based control program with higher water quality criteria and stringent environmental legislation. Additionally, in terms of residential water usage, non-governmental participation and the promotion of water conservation awareness might also be necessary.

References

1. C. Freeman, "Quenching the Dragon's Thirst:The South-North Water Transfer Project--Old Plumbing for New China?" http://www.wilsoncenter.org/publication/quenching-the-dragons-thirst-the-south-north-water-transfer-project8212old-plumbing-for (accessed on 30 September 2014).

2. China Daily, "Flow Test for Water Project Gets Underway," http://usa.chinadaily.com.cn/epaper/2013–05/31/content_16552718.htm (accessed on 13 October 2014).

3. A Total Investment of 208.6 Billion in Central Route. http://finance.sina.com.cn/china/20140704/052719605525.shtml (accessed on 10 December 2014).

4. World Bank. *China 2020: Issues and Options for China*, World Bank: Washington, DC, 1997.

5. World Bank. *Agenda for Water Sector Strategy for North China*, World Bank: Washington, DC, 2001.

6. S. Feng, L.X. Li, Z.G. Duan, and J.L. Zhang. "Assessing the Impacts of South-to-North Water Transfer Project with Decision Support Systems," *Decis. Support Syst.* 2007, *42*, 1989–2003.

7. K. Le Mentec, "The Three Gorges Dam and the Demiurges: The story of a failed contemporary myth elaboration in China," *Water Hist.* 2014, *6*, 1–19.

8. S. Barca, "Telling the right story: Environmental violence and liberation narratives," *Environ. Hist.* 2014, *20*, 535–546.

9. B. Chellaney, "Water, Power, and Competition in Asia," *Asian Surv.* 2014, *54*, 621–650.

10. K. R. James, "Policy and Planning for Large Water Infrastructure Projects in the People's Republic of China," Doctoral Dissertation, Wesleyan University, Wesleyan, CT, 2013.

11. C. He, X. He, and L. Fu, "China's South-to-North Water Transfer Project: Is it needed?" *Geogr. Compass* 2010, *4*, 1312–1323.

12. X. Chen, D. Zhang, and E. Zhang, "The South to North Water Diversions in China: Review and comments," *J. Environ. Plan. Manag.* 2002, *45*, 927–932.

13. C. Liu and H. Zheng, "South-to-North Water Transfer Schemes for China," *Int. J. Water Resour. Dev.* 2002, *18*, 453–471.

14. W. Wang, L. Gao, P. Liu, and A. Hailu, "Relationships between Regional Economic Sectors and Water Use in a Water-Scarce area in China: A quantitative analysis," *J. Hydrol.* 2014, *515*, 180–190.
15. L. Changming "Environmental issues and the south-north water transfer scheme," *China Quart.* 1998, *156*, 899–910.
16. H.S. Kim, "Sustainable development and the South-to-North Water Transfer Project in China," Doctoral Dissertation, Central Connecticut State University, New Britain, CT, 2003.
17. S. Wei, H. Yang, K. Abbaspour, J. Mousavi, A. Gnauck, "Game theory based models to analyze water conflicts in the Middle Route of the South-to-North Water Transfer Project in China," *Water Res.* 2010, *44*, 2499–2516.
18. J. Berkoff, "China: The South-North Water Transfer Project—Is it justified?" *Water Policy* 2003, *5*, 1–28.
22. W. Gu, D. Shao, and Y. Jiang, "Risk evaluation of water shortage in source area of middle route project for South-to-North Water Transfer in China," *Water Resour. Manag.* 2012, *26*, 3479–3493.
23. M. Berrittella, K. Rehdanz, R.S. Tol, *The Economic Impact of the South-North Water Transfer Project in China: A Computable General Equilibrium Analysis*, Working Papers FNU-117, Research Unit Sustainability and Global Change, Hamburg University: Hamburg, Germany, 2006.
44. D. Tang and Y. Yang, "Relationship between industrial structure and pollution density: Evidence from recent industrialization in China," *Int. J. Ecol. Dev.* 2011, *19*, 30–43.
45. National Business Daily, "Nansi Lake's Dilemma is to be Solved and the Water Rights are Not Clear," http://www.nbd.com.cn/articles/2014–08–12/855375.html (accessed on 17 November 2014).
46. J.L. Wong, "The Food-Energy-Water nexus: An integrated approach to understanding China's resource challenges," *Harv. Asia Quart.* 2010, *12*, 15–19.
47. T. Yan, J. Wang, and J. Huang, "Urbanization, agricultural water use, and regional and national crop production in China," *Ecol. Model.* 2015, *2015*.
48. R. E. Just and S. Netanyahu, *Conflict and Cooperation on Trans-Boundary Water Resources*, Kluwer Academic Publishers: Norwell, MA, 1998.
49. S. He, K. W. Hipel, and D. M. Kilgour, "Water Diversion Conflicts in China: A hierarchical perspective," *Water Resour. Manag.* 2014, *28*, 1823–1837.
50. State Council of China. Announcement on the Assessment Methods for the Most Strict Water Resource Management System. http://www.mwr.gov.cn/zwzc/zcfg/xzfghfgxwj/201301/t20130107_336155.html(accessed on 10 February 2015).
51. Water Resources Department of Jiangsu Province. The Water Resource Planning in Jiangsu Province. http://www.jswp.gov.cn/WebMain/Main/News.aspx?Id=3109 (accessed on 10 February 2015).
52. K. J. Matus, X. Xiao, and J. B. Zimmerman, "Green chemistry and green engineering in China: Drivers, policies and barriers to innovation," *J. Clean. Prod.* 2012, *32*, 193–203.
53. Bureau of Statistics of Jiangsu. *Jiangsu Statistical Yearbook 2014*, China Statistics Press: Beijing, 2014.
54. J. Y. Lin and J. Xu, "The potential for green growth and structural transformation in China," *Oxford Rev. Econ. Policy* 2014,*30*, 550–568.
55. S. M. Moore, "Modernization, authoritarianism, and the environment: The politics of China's South–North Water Transfer Project," *Environ. Politics* 2014, *23*, 1–20.
56. S. Moore, "Water Resource Issues, Policy and Politics in China; Brookings Issue Brief," http://www.brookings.edu/research/papers/2013/02/water-politics-china-moore#_edn20 (accessed on 13 March 2015).

57. China Daily, "Project Set to Deliver Clean Water Next Year," http://usa.chinadaily.com.cn/china/2012-07/26/content_15618298.htm (accessed on 13 March 2015).

58. E. C. Economy, *The River Runs Black: Environmental Challenge to China's Future*, Cornell University Press: Ithaca, NY, 2004.

59. J. Li, *The Water Ecological Civilization City Policy Conception and Explore in China*, CEWP Scientific Research Cooperation Meeting: Jinan, 2013.

60. J. Benney and P. Marolt, "Introduction: Modes of activism and engagement in the Chinese public sphere," *Asian Stud. Rev.* 2015, 39, 88–99.

61. F. Magdoff, "Ecological Civilization," *Mon. Rev.* 2011, 62, 1–25.

62. H. Yang and A. J. Zehnder, "The South-North Water Transfer Project in China: An analysis of water demand uncertainty and environmental objectives in decision making," *Water Int.* 2005, 30, 339–349.

> *"China provides the perfect example of a developing nation grappling with these urgent issues."*

It's Time to Declare War on Water Scarcity

Gabriel Wong

In the following viewpoint, Gabriel Wong highlights the multi-faceted water issues facing the nation of China, which has one of the world's largest populations. In the author's opinion, China is serving as a model for being aggressive in tackling the problem of water scarcity. The nation is one of the global leaders in desalination efforts, although desalination remains an expensive process. China is working on other fronts as well, including low-cost but effective public awareness campaigns to promote water conservation. The author suggests these initiatives should be noticed by other countries around the world. Wong leads PriceWaterhouseCoopers's infrastructure practice in China.

As you read, consider the following questions:

1. How dire is the water crisis in China?
2. Describe some of China's desalination projects and efforts.
3. How can technology alleviate water scarcity?

"China's War on Water Scarcity," by Gabriel Wong, PriceWaterhouseCoopers, 2013. Reprinted by permission.

To understand China's thirst for water, look no further than Beijing. This city of 20 million people possesses only one tenth of the world's average water resources per capita. Beijing has endured droughts each year for the past decade; its supply of surface water from reservoirs, rivers and lakes has dwindled dramatically; and its groundwater tables have dropped at a perilous rate, with water pumped out much faster than it can ever be replenished.

Beijing's chronic water shortage is emblematic of the broader challenge facing China—and, indeed, facing many water-scarce developing nations such as India, South Africa, Brazil and Turkey. In India, nearly three quarters of the population lives in water-stressed regions, yet water demand continues to surge, both for agriculture and industry. Likewise, in Brazil, soaring water demand is being driven by rapid urbanization and rising industrial use. Severe pollution has compromised the quality of the limited water supplies in these and many other emerging nations. And climate change only intensifies the uncertainty, not least by making rainfall patterns increasingly unpredictable.

China provides the perfect example of a developing nation grappling with these urgent issues. The United Nations, which lists China as one of 13 countries contending with serious water scarcity, says it has 21% of the world's population, but only 6% of its freshwater. Overall, China's per capita availability of water is just 25% of the world's average, and more than 400 Chinese cities are short of water.[1] These shortages are mostly concentrated in the parched north, which receives much less rainfall than the south.

Government planners and foreign investors alike are wrestling with the implications of these shortfalls. A 2011 HSBC report entitled China's Rising Climate Risk warns that nine Chinese provinces "suffer from extreme water scarcity." It cautions that 14 out of 31 provincial economies "could be at risk from water stress," since they rely heavily on water for everything from power generation to manufacturing. China's water shortages are further exacerbated by pollution: the World Water Organization says at least half of the country's mainstream rivers and lakes contain water unfit for human consumption, while the World Bank says 300 million people in rural China drink contaminated water daily.

With China's economy still growing at an impressive rate, water demand will only increase. But this growth requires abundant energy. The coal industry alone is expected to account for 27% of China's water use by 2020, deepening concerns about the conflicting need for energy and water.[2] Meanwhile, China's population is projected to expand from 1.3 billion to 1.45 billion by 2029, according to the Washington Post. The government thus estimates that China's water consumption will rise from 599 billion cubic meters in 2010 to 670 billion by the end of this decade.[3]

Small wonder, then, that China's leaders have made water a top priority. In March 2012, Li Keqiang—now China's Premier — warned: "Drought and water shortages are severe restrictions on the country's social and economic development."[4] Hu Siyi, China's vice minister of water resources, added: "The constraints of our available water resources become more apparent day by day… If we don't take strong measures, it will be hard to reverse the severe shortages."[5]

What measures will help? It starts with infrastructure. The most ambitious megaproject under way is a scheme to build over 2,500 kilometers of canals to carry trillions of gallons of water from the wet south to the arid north. It's ultimately expected to be the biggest construction project in history and to cost at least $60 billion. "Water transfer is very expensive," said Xiao Jincheng, a senior official at China's National Development and Reform Commission, speaking in May 2012 at a New Cities Summit in Paris. So there's also mounting pressure to conserve water. "Local governments are very strict on water usage," said Xiao. "In every city, there are water plants to treat dirty water, especially for reuse in landscaping, parks or for industrial needs." Beijing and other northern cities have already adopted water-recycling programs designed to convert wastewater into so-called "gray" water that can be used for tasks like flushing toilets and washing cars.

Aware of the mounting need to reduce pollution and use water more efficiently, the government is also investing heavily in infrastructure projects such as sewage networks and wastewater treatment plants. In their quest for greater efficiency, energy companies and utilities are also building advanced power plants that require less water to produce more electricity—an illustration of the critical role that technology must play in any country that is battling water shortages.

There is also a growing awareness in China of the need for other solutions that are relatively prosaic but highly effective. For example, public-service campaigns can be employed to encourage Chinese citizens to use water less wastefully. Likewise, collective initiatives are being explored by water companies to promote better practices among farmers, including improvements in the use of irrigation. There is also pressure to expand the use of meters in order to limit the amount of water needlessly wasted in sectors such as agriculture and industry. In addition, efficiency can be significantly enhanced simply by reducing the amount of water lost through leakage—for example, from faulty toilets and poorly-maintained sewers. These low-tech, high-impact measures are central to China's efforts to manage its water woes.

Goldman Sachs says China has seen "slow but steady growth" in water-related infrastructure over the past decade, with 89% of the population having access to "improved water facilities," versus 96% in Russia and 97% in Brazil.6 But China's need for water infrastructure remains huge. "Massive investment in water services is required in China," says the OECD, "especially in the second-level cities and in wastewater collection and treatment and pollution control."7

"We really need technology to cope with water scarcity," Xiao said at the New Cities Summit. "In future, we'll try to use desalinization of sea water." Indeed, China is already emerging as the next great market for this vital, yet controversial technology. It's easy to understand the appeal of desalination, which involves converting seawater or brackish water into freshwater. In 1961, U.S. President John F. Kennedy observed: "If we could ever competitively—at a cheap rate—get freshwater from salt water, that would be in the long-range interest of humanity, and would really dwarf any other scientific accomplishment." As the global water crisis deepens, this has become a more pressing objective, and the world is expected to produce double the quantity of desalinated water in 2016 as in 2008.

Until recently, China had merely dabbled in desalination. Compared with places like Saudi Arabia, the United Arab Emirates and Israel, its installed capacity remains meager. But the government plans to boost China's capability for producing desalinated water from about 680,000 cubic meters per day to 3 million cubic meters by 2020. The National Development and Reform Commission has assembled a team of top experts to map out China's five-year plans for the sector. Guo Youzhi, a team member who also heads the China Desalination Association, recently assured the Chinese media: "Technologies related to seawater desalination will enjoy great policy support."[8]

This government backing has sparked an international gold rush, attracting foreign firms that sell everything from miniscule components to entire desalination plants. International companies that have flocked to China include the French giant Veolia Environment, Singapore's Hyflux, America's Dow Chemical, and Norway's Aqualyng. Bullish projections abound. A 2012 report by TechSci Research predicts that China's desalination market will grow 18% annually for the next five years.[9]

What does it take for foreign companies to succeed in this highly competitive market? Few executives are as well positioned to answer that question as Avshalom Felber, CEO of the Israeli desalination company, IDE Technologies. In 2011, Global Water Intelligence named IDE as the 2010 "Desalination Company of the Year," based largely on its success in "winning a significant portion of the Chinese desalination business." IDE was specifically hailed for its "stunning project win" in Tianjin, an enormous port city about 150 kilometers from Beijing.

Tianjin is now emerging as a global showcase for the latest in desalination technology. With 10 million residents and an expanding industrial sector, it has an almost limitless need for water. Other coastal cities like Dalian and Qingdao will also drive China's desalination sector, but Tianjin has led the way, with its two biggest desalination projects accounting for as much as one third of China's total capacity.

China's largest desalination project, the Tianjin Beijiang Power and Desalination Plant, is IDE's brainchild. The state-owned investor behind it, S.D.I.C., picked IDE to provide the cutting-edge technology for this flagship project. Felber, IDE's CEO, sees the plant as part of a much broader effort by China's government "to solve the huge challenge" of water shortages in economically critical areas. "The biggest barrier to economic growth in that region, the northeast, is water scarcity," he says. "All these industries like steel mills and refiners that are very popular there are held back by lack of water."

The Persian Gulf currently accounts for 60% of the global desalination market, says Felber, but he expects China to eclipse the Gulf market within two decades. Still, nobody would suggest that it's an easy place to break in. IDE entered China in 1995, yet its breakthrough only came in 2005, with the award of the coveted contract for the Tianjin plant. After completing the first stage in 2007, IDE won a second contract in 2010 to double the plant's production capacity. "China is very centralized and political," says Felber. "A large project like this is only possible with approvals from all levels of the municipal and federal government." It was a powerful lesson on the need for a long-term perspective. "You have to be very patient and open-minded about changes that keep occurring," he says. "It's not a simple way forward."

China's government is so vast that it was difficult even to figure out who was authorized to make decisions, let alone meet with them. "It's very hard to be competitive if you don't understand what moves things, why certain decisions are taken," says Felber. "A lot of things are based on personal trust. People go with who they know. People work with their classmates. They won't do business with a person they don't like… So the biggest challenge was first to understand how they interact, how decisions are taken. This is a big issue in any country. But in China, with the language barrier, it was even harder. It's hard to understand what you're up against there, what to expect and what you can trust."

Faced with these cultural hurdles, IDE committed to become as localized as possible. All of its employees in China are Chinese. The company also joined forces with Chinese partners who understand the nuances of the local business environment. "We don't want the Chinese to play our game, or to teach them what we think is the right way to do things," says Felber. "We're trying to become Chinese ourselves."

Founded in the 1960s, IDE has built over 400 desalination plants in 40 countries as far afield as India, the U.S. and Australia. So it had a long record of innovation—and the advantage of being technologically flexible. Most of the world's desalination plants now use "membrane" technology, which typically involves a process known as reverse osmosis. This entails forcing seawater or brackish water through a semi-permeable membrane, which filters out salt crystals and other impurities. Reverse osmosis is widely viewed as the most cost-effective technology for seawater desalination. In Israel, IDE operates the world's largest reverse osmosis plants. But IDE also specializes in "thermal" desalination, which involves heating impure water and condensing the evaporated water to produce freshwater. IDE could offer both technologies to its Chinese clients, lending credibility to its advice on the best solution for Tianjin.

In the end, IDE created a version of its thermal technology for Tianjin. The city's bay is "quite highly contaminated because of the discharge of chemicals" by the industrial sector, explains Felber. "It would be very expensive and energy intensive to treat this water with membrane technology." IDE's design also incorporated an electricity plant that works in tandem with the desalination plant: the electricity plant generates waste heat, which IDE uses to power its desalination process. This cuts the energy costs of desalination, while minimizing the harmful discharge of waste heat into the atmosphere. IDE's state-ofthe-art process also takes post-desalination waste brine and recycles it to produce pure table salt. China's government has become "very environmentally aware," says Felber, and "insisted" upon a sophisticated green solution.

While Felber sees great opportunities to bring this kind of innovative technology to China, he acknowledges that it won't be easy for foreign companies to maintain their lead in the desalination industry: "The biggest challenge will be the amount of local competition. Looking from the outside, it seems too simple, so every Chinese company is asking 'Why don't we do it ourselves?' So the only way to grow in China is just to keep getting better."

In the meantime, China's desalination industry faces a fundamental economic issue: the unfeasibly low market price of desalinated water. Tech-savvy companies like IDE keep driving down the cost of producing this water, but it still remains an expensive process. The prices currently paid for desalinated water in China don't come close to reflecting the production cost. Consumers in Israel pay nearly $2 per cubic meter, says Felber, whereas Chinese consumers pay less than $1—and sometimes less than 50 cents.

China's government is eventually expected to create a more rational pricing system that better reflects the cost of desalinating water. Until then, desalination plants like IDE's project in Tianjin operate at a significant loss. The New York Times praised the Tianjin plant in October 2011 as a "technical marvel," but added that its "desalted water costs twice as much to produce as it sells for."[10]

China's state-owned companies can afford to operate this way, since they're not motivated solely by profits. Their strategic priority in a city like Tianjin is to advance the government's interest in alleviating water shortages, while also nurturing the domestic desalination industry. Foreign companies must adjust to these market dynamics. In Israel, IDE has long-term concessions to sell desalinated water to consumers; in China, its focus is exclusively on supplying desalination equipment, since the business of selling water to companies and households will remain financially unviable until the government raises water tariffs. Many argue that China's nascent desalination industry will require government subsidies until it reaches economic maturity.

While pricing may be the greatest challenge facing China's desalination sector, there's also a lingering concern that desalination may be environmentally unsound. Critics contend that the energy required in the desalination process makes it unsustainable. For China, this is a serious consideration, since most of the country's power is generated by burning coal, which emits greenhouse gases that exacerbate climate change. A carefully balanced perspective on this complex issue comes from a major study published in Science in 2011, entitled The Future of Seawater Desalination: Energy, Technology, and the Environment. While recognizing that "the carbon footprint of large-scale desalination plants can be substantial," this study notes that "continual technological improvements" have made desalination plants much more energy-efficient.

These environmental concerns—along with the relatively high cost of desalination—mean that countries suffering from water shortages must also thoroughly explore other solutions such as water conservation, water recycling and regional water transfers. But "these options alone will not be enough," concludes the report in Science. "For water-scarce countries that already implement all other measures for freshwater generation, desalination may serve as the only viable means to provide the water supply necessary to sustain agriculture, support population, and promote economic development."

China's leaders have clearly reached the same conclusion—that desalination is an indispensable weapon in their war on water scarcity. As Felber says, the Chinese government has no choice but to invest aggressively in desalination: "The scarcity is really so bad in China now that I don't see any way around it."

Notes

1. "China's Thirst for Water, Dow Water & Process Solutions," April 2011. http://www. futurewecreate.com/water/includes/ DOW072_China%20White_Opt1_Rev1.pdf

2. "How China Is Dealing With Its Water Crisis," Earth Institute at Columbia University, May 2011. http://blogs.ei.columbia.edu/2011/05/05/how-china-is-dealing-with-its-water-crisis/.

3. "Food supply, Fracking, and Water Scarcity Challenge China's Juggernaut Economy," Circle of Blue, October 2012. http://www.circleofblue.org/waternews/2012/world/choke-pointchina-ii-introduction/

4. China Daily. http://www.chinadaily.com.cn/china/2012-03/22/content_14884786.htm.

5. "China warns on growing water shortages", Financial Times, Feb 16, 2012. http://www.ft.com/cms/s/0/131bb6dc-588f-11e1-9f28-00144feabdc0.html.

6. "A Progress Report on the Building of the BRICs," Goldman Sachs, July 22, 2011.http://www.goldmansachs.com/our-thinking/topics/brics/brics-reports-pdfs/progress-onbuilding-the-brics.pdf.

7. OECD Reviews of Regulatory Reform: China 2009 —Defining the Boundary between the Market and the State, OECD, 2009.

8. "Desal in China: Trends & Opportunities, by China Water Risk," November 10, 2011. http://chinawaterrisk.org/resources/analysis-reviews/desal-in-china-trends-opportunities/

9. "China's Desalination Market," TechSci, March 2012. http://www.techsciresearch.com/1680

10. "China Takes a Loss to Get Ahead in the Business of Fresh Water", New York Times , October 25, 2011. http://www. nytimes.com/2011/10/26/world/asia/china-takes-loss-to-getahead-in-desalination-industry.html?pagewanted=all&_r=0

| "*Saving half the water, without a fussy system that needs electrical power and lots of human supervision, would be a godsend for growing crops in the desert.*"

Save Water Through Irrigation Innovation

Mary Kay Magistad

In the following viewpoint, Mary Kay Magistad describes the work of Chinese scientists who have developed new technologies and systems for making water usage more efficient in food production. The author argues that innovations such as trace irrigation and underground drip irrigation can reduce the amount of water used to supply crops. The possibility of growing crops with up to half the amount of water normally used, she continues, would drastically help improve the situation for the entire nation, since most of China's water is dedicated to the agricultural sector. Magistad is formerly The World's East Asia correspondent. She lived and reported in the region for two decades.

"Low-water lunch: A Chinese breakthrough on irrigation?" by Mary Kay Magistad, from PRI's The World, Courtesy Public Radio International, June 17, 2013. Reprinted by permission.

As you read, consider the following questions:

1. How do current Chinese agricultural practices cause water to be wasted?
2. How does the trace irrigation system work?
3. What are added benefits of trace irrigation, besides a reduction in water?

N o lunch is complete without water—the water you drink, the water that helped grow the wheat in your sandwich bread, and the water that helped grow the vegetables or meat between the slices.

China's got a problem here. It has a chronic and growing water shortage, and on the arid northern plain, where many thirsty crops are grown, the water table is plummeting, down hundreds of feet within living memory. Most of China's water use goes to agriculture, and much of that water is used inefficiently.

Surface irrigation is king in China—and on a farm on the outskirts of Beijing, a mushroom farmer is letting water gush from a hose—at high noon—onto a long raised mound of soil.

The inefficient use of water is common in China, but this is no common farm. A stone's throw away is another long, raised mound of soil, with no water source in sight. Yet, the mushrooms underneath the canvas covering are firm and healthy, and the soil is slightly moist.

The first field is the 'control'—which shows what happens when you do normal surface irrigation. The second field is trying out a new underground irrigation system, where the plants roots draw only the water they need. Gu Yunxia, the agronomist managing this project, is impressed with what the new system makes possible.

"It cuts down on pests, and fungus and weeds," she says. "We save a huge amount of water, and the vegetables also have great flavor."

This system was dubbed 'trace irrigation,' by its inventor, Beijing native and businessman Zhu Jun.

"I found if I put the chopsticks in water, and took them out, there was a little water going up between the chopsticks," he says. "And if I held the chopsticks higher, the water goes higher. And I realized, that's actually the capillary force that I learned in the textbooks in primary school. And maybe that is a good way for irrigation."

Capillary force, for those who might be rusty on what they learned in school, is when molecules are so attracted to each other that they can pull liquid against the force of gravity—kind of the way a kerosene lamp works. In this case, it's the roots of a plant pulling water, and when they have enough, they stop pulling.

This system uses PV pipes, buried a foot or even deeper in soil. The pipes get narrower, and narrower, until they're like thin straws, with something that looks like a tiny showerhead at the end, with little white threads coming out of it. These pipes are buried in the soil – and the plant sucks the moisture it needs from these threads.

Zhu says, he has worked on this system for about a decade. Before that, he'd worked on a technology called "dry water"— encasing water droplets in silicon. A couple of pounds of the stuff is enough to grow a tree in a desert for 100 days—one of many solutions that the world's scientists have been busy developing, to cope with a growing global water shortage.

Another is underground drip irrigation—similar to Zhu's system, but with a recurring problem. He says, in such systems, there's a small and irregular flow of water, so pipes can easily get clogged. And that's been a limit on the otherwise revolutionary technology of drip irrigation that Israel first introduced decades ago.

"I found that if the capillary pipe gets too small, no matter how you purify the water, the particles in the water will still block the pipe," he says. "That was a bottleneck for me, for awhile."

Eventually, he experimented with a double-membrane to filter particles, and found a combination that wouldn't clog, even with very low water pressure. That's one of the innovations for which he's seeking patents.

Zhu says his system saves 70 or more of the water used in surface irrigation in China, and 30 to 50 percent compared to drip irrigation. Those are big claims, says Bob von Bernuth, the education director of the US Irrigation Association.

"Well, I guess anytime someone claims to save 50 percent of water, especially over drip irrigation, one becomes immediately skeptical," von Bernuth says. "I can tell you that it's possible, but unlikely....it suggests they weren't doing a very good job of saving water to begin with."

In China, that's true. Many farmers don't consider the true cost of the water they're using, because they just divert rivers or drill wells to get it, so they often don't use water efficiently.

And in China, there's been significant interest in Zhu's new system. He has already received two patents in China and one in New Zealand and Japan for trace irrigation, and he has applications pending in dozens of other countries, including the United States. Von Bernuth reviewed Zhu's US patent application, and said it doesn't seem that different from underground drip technology already in use. But Zhu Jun says it is, and local Chinese governments are keenly interested.

Beijing's municipal Science & Technology Commission, and its Municipal Agriculture Commission started doing their own trace irrigation trials six years ago, liked the results, and invested. The city of Wuhan has offered him land to build a factory, and the government of Xinjiang—one of China's driest regions—is now growing test crops. If all goes well, they plan to use the system on a larger scale next year. Saving half the water, without a fussy system that needs electrical power and lots of human supervision, would be a godsend for growing crops in the desert.

Meanwhile, Kim Ji-Seok, a Korean agronomist, was so intrigued by this new technology that he left his job with agribusiness giant Syngenta to join Zhu company Puquan—which means 'spreading spring.' He takes me for a tour around the experimental farm on the edge of Beijing – past walnut groves, peach trees, corn, cotton and peanut fields.

"The government is quite excited about the result last year," he says. Excited enough to greenlight bigger scale trials—growing grapes, watermelon, jujubes, and licorice.

And Kim's excited too. It's not so often an agronomist gets to work on what just might prove to be a game-changing technology that could help solve one of China's—and the world's—biggest problems—lack of adequate water—and maybe one or two other problems, to boot.

We walk into a greenhouse, with rain pattering overhead. One section of the greenhouse—which uses drip irrigation—feels humid. The other section, using trace irrigation, doesn't. Kim says, that's because there's less water in the soil to evaporate up.

"In this way, the diseases decrease," he says. "So we use less pesticides, less fungicides than drip line."

And half as much fertilizer, too. If the 'trace irrigation' system is used on a large scale throughout China, that would be good news for China's lakes and rivers and groundwater, now choked with agricultural runoff.

Kim also shows off how uniformly attractive the vegetables on the trace irrigation side of the greenhouse are, compared to those using drip irrigation.

"If you use a drip line, the first one (along the line) is very big and tasty," he says. But then they get smaller, and at the end, you get a tiny one. If it's not uniform, you cannot sell them."

It's time to break for lunch, and Kim suggests we start with crudités—a little trace irrigation-grown celery. I crunch into mine and declare it delicious. Kim grins broadly. And if this is a taste of things to come in China, growing better produce with less fertilizer, pesticide and much less water, there's certainly something to smile about.

Periodical and Internet Sources Bibliography

The following articles have been selected to supplement the diverse views presented in this chapter.

Michael Beach, "Safe Water Saves Lives: World Water Day 2013." https://blogs.cdc.gov/global/2013/03/18/world-water-day2013.

Damian Carrington, "Four Billion People Face Severe Water Scarcity, New Research Finds," Guardian, February 12, 2016. https://www.theguardian.com/environment/2016/feb/12/four-billion-people-face-severe-water-scarcity-new-research-finds.

Rowan Jacobsen, "Israel Proves the Desalination Era is Here," Scientific American, July 29, 2016. https://www.scientificamerican.com/article/israel-proves-the-desalination-era-is-here.

Karen Klein, "Water Desalination Is Here, but Is It Sustainable?" Los Angeles Times, October 20, 2015. http://www.latimes.com/opinion/livable-city/la-ol-desalination-20151019-story.html.

Lori Lewis, "Rural and Urban Water Issues in Africa." https://thewaterproject.org/pdf/rural-and-urban-water-issues-africa.pdf.

Population Institute, "Population and Water," July 2010. https://www.populationinstitute.org/external/files/Fact_Sheets/Water_and_population.pdf.

Alistair Sinclair, "South Africa's Water Crisis Is about More Than Droughts and Restrictions," Huffington Post, January 10, 2017. http://www.huffingtonpost.co.za/alastair-sinclair/south-africas-water-crisis-is-about-more-than-droughts-and-rest.

David Talbot, "Desalination Out of Desperation," December 16, 2014, MIT Technology Review. https://www.technologyreview.com/s/533446/desalination-out-of-desperation.

Tamsin Woolley-Barker, "The Biomimicry Manual: What Can a Thorny Devil Teach Us About Water Harvesting?" Inhabitat. http://inhabitat.com/the-biomimicry-manual-what-can-a-thorny-devil-teach-us-about-water-harvesting.

World Water Council, "Water Crisis: Towards a Way to Improve the Situation." http://www.worldwatercouncil.org/library/archives/water-crisis.

For Further Discussion

Chapter 1:

1. How does a lack of clean, safe water contribute to poverty, women's issues, and human rights issues?
2. How severe is the water scarcity crisis in the Western Hemisphere? The Eastern Hemisphere?
3. What are the various ways in which the water crisis is apparent (floods, droughts, contaminated water, poor infrastructure, etc)?

Chapter 2:

1. How quickly has the global population grown in the past ten years? Twenty years? Which countries have the highest population numbers?
2. Why has fracking become such a contentious issue? Do you think it harms the environment and water availability, or is it a sustainable practice?
3. What can be done to slow down the rate of global warming? What can companies, governments, communities, and individuals do?

Chapter 3:

1. Which regions of the world are most volatile in terms of political problems caused by water issues?
2. Does a nation "own" the rights to water in its region? Can water bodies be claimed in this way?
3. In which ways can water be used as a weapon against another country?

Chapter 4:

1. Do you think desalination is a sustainable technology? What are the pros and cons?
2. Are there other examples (in addition to the Thorny Devil) of nature's conservation of water that humans can imitate as biomimicry?
3. What are the legal and ethical implications of trying to limit population growth?

Organizations to Contact

The editors have compiled the following list of organizations concerned with the issues debated in this book. The descriptions are derived from materials provided by the organizations. All have publications or information available for interested readers. The list was compiled on the date of publication of the present volume; the information provided here may change. Be aware that many organizations take several weeks or longer to respond to inquiries, so allow as much time as possible.

Miya Action Group
46A. Avenue J.F Kennedy, L-1855 Luxembourg
972-3-777-9800
email: Info@miya-water.com
website: http://www.miya-water.com/

Miya works to maximize the efficiency of water utilities as a way of preventing water waste. Many cities have old pipes and infrastructure which leads to water that is wasted before it ever reaches consumers.

National Water Research Institute
18700 Ward Street, Fountain Valley, CA 92708
Phone: 714-378-3278
website: http://www.nwri-usa.org/index.htm

The NWRI is a nonprofit organization that works to ensure safe sources of water.

Soil and Water Conservation Society
945 SW Ankeny Road, Ankeny, IA 50023-9723
Phone: 515-289-2331
website: http://www.swcs.org/

SWCS is a nonprofit scientific and educational organization with over 3000 members. It works to research and advocate for water conservation practice, programs, and policy.

Union of Concerned Scientists
Two Brattle Sq., Cambridge, MA 02138-3780
Phone: 617-547-5552
website: http://www.ucsusa.org/

The Union of Concerned Scientists works to apply scientific research to promote awareness of the dangers of climate change.

The United Nations
Department of Economic and Social Affairs (UNDESA)
405 East 42nd Street, New York, NY, 10017
Phone: 212-963-8652
email: water-decade@un.org
website: http://www.un.org/waterforlifedecade/index.shtml

The United Nations Department of Economic and Social Affairs (UNDESA) sponsored the International Water for Life Decade program, from 2005-2015, to help nations understand and reach their goals for water-related issues.

US Army Corps of Engineers
441 G Street NW, Washington, DC 20314-1000
Phone: 202-761-0011
website: http://www.usace.army.mil/

The US Army Corps of Engineers is an agency of over 37,000 civilian and miltary scientists who serve the needs of people in over 130 countries.

Water.org
117 West 20th Street, Suite 203, Kansas City, MO, 64108-1909
Phone: 816-877-8451
email: donorcare@water.org
website: http://www.water.org

Water.org is an organization that works to bring safe and sanitary drinking water to areas that are affected by poverty.

The Water Project
The Water Project, PO Box 3353, Concord, NH 03302-3353
Phone: 800-460-8974
email: info@thewaterproject.org
website: https://thewaterproject.org/

The Water Project is a research and community service organization that seeks to educate people about the lack of fresh, safe water that exists in many regions of the world.

Water Research Foundation
6666 West Quincy Avenue, Denver, CO 80235-3098
Phone: 303-347-6100
email: Info@WaterRF.org
website: http://www.waterrf.org/Pages/Index3.aspx

The Water Research Foundation promotes scientific and industrial ways to make drinking water safe and available.

World Water Forum
+55 (61) 3961-5079
email: esecretariat@adasa.df.gov.br
website: http://www.worldwaterforum8.org/

The World Water Forum is a major international conference organized by the World Water Council (WWC). Its website includes helpful resources.

Bibliography of Books

Marta Antonelli and Francesca Greco. *The Water We Eat: Combining Virtual Water and Water Footprints*. New York, NY: Springer Publishing, 2016

Shlomi Dinar and Ariel Dinar. *International Water Scarcity and Variability: Managing Resource Use Across Political Boundaries*. Oakland, CA: University of California Press, 2016.

Saeid Eslamian and Faezeh A. Eslamian. *Handbook of Drought and Water Scarcity: Environmental Impacts and Analysis of Drought and Water*. Boca Raton, FL: CRC Press, 2017

Charles Fishman. *The Big Thirst: The Secret Life and Turbulent Future of Water*. Florence, MA: Free Press, 2012.

Robert Glennon. *Unquenchable: America's Water Crisis and What To Do About It*. Washington, DC: Island Press, 2010.

B. Lynn Ingram and Frances Malamud-Roam. *The West without Water: What Past Floods, Droughts, and Other Climatic Clues Tell Us about Tomorrow*. Oakland, CA: University of California Press, 2015.

Cathryn Berger Kaye and Philippe Cousteau. *Going Blue: A Teen Guide to Saving Our Oceans, Lakes, Rivers, & Wetlands*. Minneapolis, MN: Free Spirit Publishing, 2010.

Toby Craig Jones. *Running Dry: Essays on Energy, Water, and Environmental Crisis*. New Brunswick, NJ: Rutgers University Press, 2015.

David E Newton. *The Global Water Crisis: A Reference Handbook*. Goleta, CA: ABC-CLIO, 2016.

Girgio Osti. *Storage and Scarcity: New Practices for Food, Energy and Water*. London, UK: Routledge, 2016.

Brian Richter. *Chasing Water: A Guide for Moving from Scarcity to Sustainability.* Washington, DC: Island Press, 2014.

Manoj Roy and Sally Cawood. *Urban Poverty and Climate Change: Life in the Slums of Asia, Africa and Latin America.* London, UK: Routledge, 2016.

James Salzman. *Drinking Water: A History.* New York, NY: Overlook Press, 2013.

David Sedlak. *Water 4.0: The Past, Present, and Future of the World's Most Vital Resource.* New Haven, CT: Yale University Press, 2015.

Vandana Shiva. *Water Wars: Privatization, Pollution, and Profit.* Berkeley, CA: North Atlantic Books, 2016.

Shweta Sinha. *Why Should I Save Water?: A Smart Kid's Guide to a Green World.* New Delhi, India: The Energy and Resources Institute, 2016.

Steven Solomon. *Water: The Epic Struggle for Wealth, Power, and Civilization.* New York, NY: Harper Perennial, 2011.

Pierre Thielbörger. *The Right(s) to Water: The Multi-Level Governance of a Unique Human Right.* New York, NY: Springer 2016.

Cecilia Tortajada and Choon Nam Ong. *Water Reuse Policies for Potable Use.* London, UK: Routledge, 2017.

World Bank. *Renewable Energy Desalination: An Emerging Solution to Close the Water Gap in the Middle East and North Africa.* Washington, DC: World Bank Publications, 2012.

Index

A

Africa, 24, 40-42, 58, 103, 126-132, 140-141
agriculture,
  conservation methods, 25, 91-93, 107-108, 132
  pollution from, 22-23, 30, 32, 81, 93, 180
  water use, 21, 32, 48, 75, 79, 91, 130-131
  see also irrigation
algae blooms, 29
Almaty Agreement, 113
Amu Darya, 112
armed conflict, 102, 103-104, 112-114, 126

B

biomimicry, 144-146
bottled water industry, 29
Brazil, 167

C

California, 32-33, 44-52, 58-60, 100, 104
carbon emissions, 86
children and families, 22, 42, 114, 142
China, 24, 55, 59, 60-61, 67, 71-75, 97, 153-163, 167-174, 177-180
cholera, 28, 41, 126, 131
cisterns, 123, 124
climate change, 61, 64-68, 73, 86, 90, 140, 167

contaminated drinking water, 61, 80-82, 90, 100, 168
contraception, 64, 142
Cote d'Ivoire, 126

D

dams, 97, 103, 112-114, 116-120, 127, 131
Darfur, 126-127
desalination, 25, 47, 103, 148-151, 170-174
disease, 17, 28, 41, 86-87, 90, 126, 131, 140
drinking water requirements, 106-107, 138-142
drought, 45-52, 73, 90, 100, 108, 130, 168

E

economic development, 20, 61, 66, 72, 126, 129, 130, 168, 174
Egypt, 24, 103
energy demands and production, 41, 58-62, 79-80, 101, 104, 116-120, 167
environmental impact, 50-51, 72, 77, 82, 107, 149
Ethiopia, 103

F

Flint, MI, 17, 28-29, 33
Florida, 35
food production, 23, 86-87, 90-91, 92-93, 107-108, 123-124, 139, 142, 156, 177-180

G

Ganges River, 23, 88, 107
Georgia, 33
Ghana, 40-42
glaciers, 23, 65, 86, 90, 140
Grace satellite records, 100, 101
groundwater aquifers and
   depletion, 20-23, 61, 75, 77-84,
   101, 102, 104, 139, 180

H

human rights, 31, 35-38, 87, 113
hydraulic fracturing ("fracking"),
   58-62, 101
hydropower, 116-120, 130

I

India, 23, 86-88, 97, 102, 106-110,
   116-120, 167
industrial water use, 21-22, 38, 81-
   82, 86-87, 167
infrastructure, 30, 32, 40-41, 47,
   127, 153-163, 168-169
Interferometric Synthetic Aperture
   Radar (InSAR), 71, 78-79
International Court of Arbitration
   (ICA), 116-118
Iowa, 32
Iran, 103
Iraq, 101-102
irrigation, 21, 25, 91-92, 101, 132,
   142, 177-180
Israel, 24, 97, 122-124

J

Japan, 23
Jordan, 24, 97, 103

K

Kazakhstan, 112-114
Klamath River, 51
Kyrgyzstan, 112-114

L

lakes, 23
landscaping, 35, 49, 55-56
lead poisoning, 17

M

Massachusetts, 29-30
Mekong River, 24
monsoon forecasting, 108

N

natural gas, 58-62
New York City, 29-30
Niger River, 24
Nile River, 24, 103

P

Pakistan, 97, 102, 116-120
Palestinian territory, 97, 122-124
political stability, 97-98, 102, 126
pollution, 22-23, 29, 32-33, 59, 81-
   82, 107, 108-109, 167-168
population growth, 20, 61, 64-68,
   87, 107, 138-142
private sector suppliers, 25-26, 33,
   35-38, 41, 47, 87
public service campaigns, 169
public water management, 25-26,
   29-33, 47, 87-88, 104

R

rainfall and rainwater, 88, 90, 92, 103, 108, 124
rationing, 35, 103
refugees, 103
religious beliefs, 31, 36, 37-38, 109
renewable energy, 60, 145, 150-151
rivers, 23, 24, 86, 108-109, 116-120, 180
Rome, 36

S

salt contamination, 50, 82
Salton Sea, 49-50
saltwater, 72
sanitation, 87, 109, 130, 131, 140
siphoning, 40-41
South-to-North Water Diversion Project (China), 153-163
storage and distribution systems, 75, 123-124, 146
subsidence, 71-75, 77, 78-79, 83-84
Syr Darya, 112

T

Tajikistan, 112-114
taxation, 32, 97, 163
terrorism, 102, 103, 117
trace irrigation, 177-180

U

United Arab Emirates, 103
United Kingdom, 100
United Nations Environmental Program (UNEP), 22, 24, 127
urbanization issues, 28, 48-49, 71, 74-75, 101, 167
Uzbekistan, 112-114

W

wastewater recycling, 149, 168-169
water conservation methods and programs, 25, 26, 28, 47, 86, 123, 132, 141-142, 146, 163, 169
water quality permit trading, 163
water supply safety, 28, 29, 30, 126, 127, 131, 140-141
water transfer programs, 45-46, 48, 49-50, 74-75, 153-163
wildlife, 49-50, 51, 59, 83, 146, 149

Y

Yangtze River, 162
Yellow River, 86, 153